The Plant Protein *Revolution* Cookbook

Supercharge Your Body with
More Than 85 Delicious Vegan
Recipes Made with Protein-Rich
Plant-Based Ingredients

ROBIN ROBERTSON

Bestselling author of
One-Dish Vegan and *Vegan Planet*

HARVARD
COMMON
PRESS

Brimming with creative inspiration, how-to projects, and useful information to enrich your everyday life, Quarto Knows is a favorite destination for those pursuing their interests and passions. Visit our site and dig deeper with our books into your area of interest: Quarto Creates, Quarto Cooks, Quarto Homes, Quarto Lives, Quarto Drives, Quarto Explores, Quarto Gifts, or Quarto Kids.

First Published in 2020 by
The Harvard Common Press, an imprint of The Quarto Group,
100 Cummings Center, Suite 265-D, Beverly, MA 01915, USA.
T (978) 282-9590 F (978) 283-2742 QuartoKnows.com

The Harvard Common Press titles are also available at discount for retail, wholesale, promotional, and bulk purchase. For details, contact the Special Sales Manager by email at specialsales@quarto.com or by mail at The Quarto Group, Attn: Special Sales Manager, 100 Cummings Center, Suite 265-D, Beverly, MA 01915, USA.

24 23 22 21 20   2 3 4 5 6

ISBN: 978-1-59233-960-0

Digital edition published in 2020
eISBN: 978-1-63159-890-6

Library of Congress Cataloging-in-Publication Data

Robertson, Robin (Robin G.) author.
Plant protein revolution cookbook : supercharge your body with more
   than 85 delicious vegan recipes made with protein-rich plant-based
   ingredients / Robin Robertson.
ISBN 9781592339600 (paperback) | ISBN 9781631598906 (ebook)
1. Proteins in human nutrition. 2. Plant proteins as food. 3. Diet. 4. Cookbooks.
LCC TX553.P7 R63 2020 (print) | LCC TX553.P7 (ebook) |
   DDC 613.2/82--dc23

LCCN 2020003975 (print) | LCCN 2020003976 (ebook)

Design: www.traffic-design.co.uk
Page Layout: www.traffic-design.co.uk
Photography: Jackie Sobon

Printed in USA

For the animals

Contents

The Plant Protein Revolution

Ever since I first began eating a plant-based diet (more than thirty years ago), the first question I am asked is, "Where do you get your protein?"

This question comes out of a long-held myth in our society that eating animals is necessary to ensure adequate protein consumption. Nothing could be further from the truth. What is true is that you can get all the protein you need (and more) by eating a whole-food plant-based diet. Consider the plants-only diet of the strongest, most muscular animals in nature, such as the gorilla, elephant, and horse. Many of our elite athletes are following suit, as more and more of them discover that plant-based diets give them a winning edge.

The bottom line is eating meat isn't required by the human body to supply enough protein. In fact, studies show that people can actually eat too much animal protein, whereas plant foods supply amino acids the body uses without causing an imbalance.

Eliminating meat also reduces the risk of a number of health issues, but it doesn't reduce your ability to enjoy a satisfying meal. Still, the myth that plants can't supply enough protein remains one of the main reasons that people still include meat on their plates. I hope this book will help change that as people discover how easy and delicious it can be to get all the protein you need from the plants you eat.

The focus of *The Plant Protein Revolution Cookbook* is about good eating in eighty-five delicious recipes that I have developed to provide maximum plant-based protein, along with all the other nutrients that meatless and dairy-free whole foods contain. You will see for yourself how easy and delicious it can be to get all the protein you need from the plants you eat.

The recipes in this book feature protein-rich ingredients in various delicious combinations to maximize your protein intake throughout the day. Along the way you will discover just how much essential protein is packed into recipes such as Black Bean Enchiladas (page 130), Noodle Salad with Edamame and Sesame Dressing (page 62), Chili-Cheesy Baked Potatoes (page 123), African Peanut Stew with Red Beans and Sweet Potatoes (page 102), and many other tantalizing dishes that will keep you satisfied throughout the day. There are even protein-packed desserts, such as Almond Butter Blondies (page 157) and Blueberry Chia Pudding (page 162), to satisfy your sweet tooth.

Much of the western world has awakened to the dangers of meat and dairy consumption. Statistics show that eating plant-based protein continues to rise, as indicated by the increasing number of plant-powered celebrities, the soaring success of plant-based food companies, and the rise in people adopting a plant-based diet for reasons of health, ethics, and the environment.

We see this growing interest in vegan offerings in hospitals and school lunch programs. We see it in the fast-food industry, where chains now offer plant-based burgers and nuggets. We see it in the growth of vegan restaurants worldwide, as well as in our own cities. We see it in the condemnation of meat-centered diets by the American Medical Association, the World Health Organization, and others.

The evidence is clear that we're in the midst of a plant-protein revolution. This book hopes to put to rest that old meat-promotion protein myth. From now on, when someone asks how you get your protein, you can confidently say, "I get my protein from plants. Don't you?" *Vive la revolution!*

Chapter 1
All about Plant Protein

Before we dig into the delicious recipes,
let's talk about this thing called protein.

Simply put, protein is essential throughout the body,
because it builds muscle, bone, skin, hair, and
virtually every other body part or tissue. Chemically,
proteins are made up of amino acids, many of which
are produced naturally in our bodies. The rest, we
must get daily from our food, because our bodies
don't store these amino acids, like they do fats and
carbs. We can see the effects of severe protein
deficiency in famine-stricken countries.

The good news about protein is that we can get all
the protein we need from plant-based foods. The bad
news is, many people aren't aware of this, resulting in
a myth that perpetuates the notion that plant-based
foods don't have protein or don't have complete
proteins. How can this be?

The Protein Myth

Longtime vegans will tell you that hardly a day goes by without someone asking, "How do you get your protein?" The probable origin for this myth is both a historic lack of interest in responsible analysis of plant-based nutrition and disinformation promoted by our own government and the meat and dairy industries.

Even now, the NIH Medline Plus web page states that "Proteins from meat and other animal products are complete proteins. This means they supply all of the amino acids the body can't make on its own. Most plant proteins are incomplete. ..." However, the NIH also links to guidelines of the Harvard School of Public Health: *Get your protein from plants when possible.*

Plant-based nutrition authorities, along with the World Health Organization and the American Medical Association, finally agree that we don't require animal flesh to get all the amino acids that we need. Much research shows that we can get it all with a plant-based diet.

Because this is a cookbook, I'll spare you the scientific jargon, but you can educate yourself on plant protein by reading books such as *The China Study* by T. Colin Campbell and Thomas Campbell and other books by Neal Barnard, M.D., Joel Fuhrman, M.D., and Michael Greger, M.D. (See Further Reading, page 186, for more information.)

Food Allergies

A quick look at the plant foods that are especially protein-rich shows that soy foods, seitan (wheat-meat), beans, and nuts and seeds have the highest levels. While there are people who may have allergies to one or more of these foods, the solution is simple: use the plant protein sources you *can* eat. If you can't eat soy, substitute beans or seitan instead and use coconut aminos instead of tamari. If you are gluten intolerant, skip the seitan but eat a variety of beans and soy foods. The same holds true for nut allergies. If you're allergic to peanuts, use cashews, almonds, or sunflower seeds instead.

How Much Protein Do We Need?

It's imperative that we get enough daily protein. The recommended daily allowance (RDA) depends on various factors, including gender, state of health, age, and how active you are. People in the United States, the United Kingdom, and other industrialized countries do consume enough protein, though many, mostly meat eaters, overdo it, and too much protein can be harmful.

However, getting enough protein on a plant-based diet is actually quite simple. All you need to do is eat a healthy, whole foods, plant-based diet that includes grains, legumes, vegetables, fruit, leafy greens, and small amounts of healthy fats like nuts, seeds, and avocado. That's it.

Most people generally don't need to track their protein intake. If you're a healthy person trying to stay healthy, then simply eating a balanced, whole-food, plant-based diet should bring your intake to an optimal range. The RDA of protein for an average, healthy person is 7 grams of protein for every 20 pounds (9 kg) of the person's body weight. We can achieve this by eating a diet that is between 10 and 35 percent protein over the course of a day. Athletes, pregnant and breastfeeding women, older adults, and people who do physically demanding jobs need more.

According to the National Academy of Medicine (NAM), the daily RDA for protein is as follows:

- Males, 19 to 70 years and older: 56 to 90 grams per day
- Females, 14 to 70 years and older: 46 to 75 grams per day

Based on recent findings, some experts now recommend that moderately active people and older adults increase their protein to about 20 percent of their calories, or 0.45 to 0.54 grams per pound of ideal body weight. This translates to 68 to 81 grams of protein per day.

To achieve those goals, most meals should contain a minimum of 15 to 20 grams of protein. These amounts are said to also improve appetite control and weight management. Not enough protein may leave you feeling hungry shortly after a meal, while eating too much might cause digestive upset or trigger the release of too much insulin in the body.

If you have questions about how much protein you need, discuss it with a doctor, nutritionist, or other medical professional, preferably one who is educated in plant-based nutrition. If you're looking for a medical professional versed in plant-based nutrition or information on maintaining a healthy plant-based diet, I highly recommend contacting Barnard Medical Center in Washington, D.C.

Protein Plus

All of the recipes in this book are rich in protein, but some contain more protein than others. To help you find the recipes that are super high in protein, look for the Protein Plus icon on pages with recipes containing 15 grams of protein or more per serving.

PROTEIN PLUS

Why Choose Plant-Based Proteins over Animal Proteins?

A plant-powered diet makes more sense than one based on animals in four important ways.

1. Health reasons

According to numerous research studies, including those from the Harvard School of Public Health, a plant-based diet can help ward off chronic diseases, such as diabetes, kidney disease, and some cancers. It can help with weight loss, reduce the risk of heart disease and hypertension, lower cholesterol, prevent constipation, and improve skin health.

2. Environmental reasons

Many of the root problems associated with the current environmental and world hunger crises can be traced to animal agriculture. For example, 60 percent of all water used in America is used for meat production; since the late 1960s, forests have been destroyed at a rate of 1 acre (0.4 hectare) every 5 seconds to create grazing land for beef cattle; runoff from animal waste is linked to a 7,000-square-mile (18,129 sq km) dead zone in the Gulf of Mexico; it takes 16 pounds (7.25 kg) of grain and 2,500 gallons (9,464 L) of water to produce 1 pound (455 g) of meat.

3. Ethical reasons

The realities of animal agriculture are more shockingly cruel and horrendous than most of us can imagine. Eating a plant-based diet can help end the needless suffering and deaths of millions of animals.

4. Wait, there's more...

As if you need more reasons to skip the meat and eat the plants: it can also save you money, both in the food you buy, as well as less frequent medical bills. Oh yes, and another thing: when cooked properly, plant-powered foods can taste great and be deeply satisfying.

So eating plant food is good for my health, the planet, animals, and saves me money? Like I said, a plant-based diet makes sense.

Plants Are Rich in Protein

The question of whether plant-based diets provide enough protein is easily put to rest with another question: "Where do the animals get their protein?" When you think of the biggest, strongest animals on the planet such as elephants, giraffes, horses, buffalo, cows, or gorillas, they don't eat meat. They eat what grows out of the ground, and that is where they get their protein; it's as simple as that. Plants are their source of protein.

Many foods in the plant kingdom are especially rich in protein. All the legume family—anything that grows in a pod, such as lentils, beans, and chickpeas—and whole grains are full of protein, and many vegetables are rich in protein, too. Animal meat is not required to build muscle or bone.

Plants are high-energy foods, and it's interesting to note that an increasing number of athletes are switching to a vegan diet. Recent winners of long-distance events like triathlons, marathons, and bicycle races eat a vegan diet. These athletes recognize that with a diverse, plant-based diet, they get injured less often, recover more quickly, and have more stamina.

Complete Protein vs. Incomplete Protein

Because most individual plant foods, such as whole grains, legumes, and vegetables, contain varying amounts of essential amino acids, they are said to be "incomplete proteins." There are a few exceptions, such as the soybean, which contains an abundance of all nine essential amino acids and is, therefore, a "complete protein."

It was once thought that certain foods, such as beans and grains, needed to be carefully combined at the same meal in order to make a complete protein. In recent years, we have learned that is not the case. Beans, grains, and other wholesome plant-based ingredients can be eaten throughout the day (not necessarily at the same meal) and they will have the same benefits as if they were "combined" (or eaten together). The fact is, because grains and beans are frequently paired together in scores of tasty dishes, they are often enjoyed at the same meal anyway.

High-Protein Plant Foods

It's reasonable to ask how plants can provide sufficient protein, as well as all the other nutrients that you need. The fact is, certain plant foods contain significantly more protein than others. And higher-protein diets can promote muscle strength, satiety, and weight loss. Among the most protein-rich plant foods are beans and legumes, whole grains, nuts and seeds, seitan (wheat meat), and soy foods. Fresh produce also contains protein in varying degrees, with most vegetables containing more protein than fruit.

In an effort to provide the most protein-rich recipes, this book concentrates on the plant-foods at the upper levels of protein content. Below are some of the protein-rich plant foods that are featured in this book, including some that you may surprise you.

- Beans and legumes
- Soy foods: tofu, tempeh, edamame
- Grains
- Nuts
- Seeds
- Nut and seed butters
- Many vegetables and fruits
- Nutritional yeast

For more detailed information about these protein-rich foods, read on.

Nutritional Yeast

Nutritional yeast is a deactivated yeast, sold commercially as a yellow powder or flakes. This complete source of plant protein provides the body with 14 grams of protein and 7 grams of fiber per ounce (28 g). Because it has a rich cheese-like flavor, nutritional yeast is often used to make plant-based mac & cheese, queso dip, and other cheesy foods. It can be mixed into dishes, soups, sauces, and dressings, or sprinkled on pasta, grain, or veggie dishes to boost the protein content even higher. It also makes a great topping for popcorn.

Spirulina

Spirulina, a blue-green algae, is a nutritious high-protein food with many beneficial health-enhancing properties. Just 2 tablespoons (14 g) contain 8 grams of complete protein, in addition to providing 22 percent of your daily requirements of iron and thiamin and 42 percent of your daily copper needs. Spirulina is also rich in nutrients, such as iron, magnesium, riboflavin, and manganese.

Beans and Legumes

Beans of all kinds provide an inexpensive source of protein, and bean dishes are easy to prepare. They are low in fat and an important component of a well-balanced, plant-based diet. The most popular varieties of beans and legumes are chickpeas, lentils, black beans, black-eyed peas, pintos, kidney beans, lima beans, and cannellini beans. Kidney, black, pinto, and most other varieties of beans contain great amounts of protein per serving. Most beans contain about 15 grams of protein per cooked cup (235 ml). With the exception of lentils and split peas, all dried beans require soaking. Soaking rehydrates the beans and shortens their cooking time. It also dissolves some of the complex sugars that cause digestive gas. Be sure to pick through them first in order to remove small stones, and other debris.

To soak beans, place them in a bowl with enough water to cover them by 3 inches (7.5 cm). Soak them overnight and drain before cooking. To quick-soak beans, put them in a pot under 2 to 3 inches (5 to 7.5 cm) of water and boil for 2 minutes. Remove the pot from the stove, cover it, and let it stand for 2 hours. Drain the beans, and they're ready for cooking.

Beans can be cooked in a pressure cooker, multi-cooker, slow cooker, oven, or on the stovetop. Since I'm trying to limit the special equipment used in this book, here's a simple way to cook beans on the stovetop: Soak 1 cup (250g) of beans overnight, then drain. In a large saucepan, combine the beans and 3 cups (710 ml) of fresh water and salt, if using. Simmer until tender. Cooking times will vary, usually ranging from 1 to 3 hours, depending on the type, quality, and age of the beans. Altitude and even water quality can also influence the cooking time. The yield for 1 cup (250 g) of dried beans is 2 to 2½ cups (475 to 590 ml) of cooked beans. The protein content per serving of beans varies according to the type of bean (see chart on page 26) and averages about 15 grams per serving.

Soy Foods:
Tofu, Tempeh, and Edamame

Tofu, tempeh, and edamame are all derived from the soybean, which is a source of complete protein. They are among the richest sources of protein in a plant-based diet and can be prepared in a variety of ways.

Tofu

A versatile ingredient and good source of protein, tofu has the ability to absorb the flavors that surround it. Also known as bean curd, tofu is made from ground, cooked soybeans in a process similar to cheese-making. Tofu is available in two main types: regular (Chinese) and silken (Japanese). Both types come in three textures: soft, firm, and extra-firm. Extra-firm regular tofu is the sturdiest of the two main types. The firm and extra-firm varieties are ideal in stir-fries and other dishes in which the tofu must retain its shape. Regular tofu is most often packed in water-filled tubs, so before using it in a recipe, it is essential to drain off the water. Silken tofu, or Japanese-style tofu, is used when you want a smooth and creamy result, such as in smoothies, sauces, and puddings.

Tempeh

Tempeh is made by cooking and slightly fermenting mature soybeans prior to pressing them into a slab. Originating in Indonesia, tempeh is high in protein with a chewy texture. Tempeh can be found in the refrigerated or freezer sections of natural foods stores, Asian markets, and some supermarkets. It can be sliced lengthwise to make thin slices and can also be cut into strips or cubes, or grated. Tempeh marinates well and turns a crisp golden brown when sautéed. Tempeh will keep, unopened, in the refrigerator for several weeks (check the expiration date). Once it is opened, however, it should be wrapped tightly and used within 3 days. Tempeh will keep for a month or so frozen. As tempeh can have a strong nutty flavor, steaming it for 20 minutes will mellow the flavor and improve digestibility.

Edamame

Edamame are immature soybeans with a sweet and slightly grassy taste. They need to be steamed or boiled prior to consumption and can be eaten on their own or added to soups and salads. Soybeans are considered a source of complete protein. This means that they provide the body with all the essential amino acids it needs. Edamame are also rich in folate, vitamin K, and fiber.

Soy Milk

Soy milk is a high-protein plant-based milk. It is made from soybeans, fortified with vitamins, contains 7 grams of protein per cup (235 ml), and is also an excellent source of calcium, vitamin D, and vitamin B12. However, keep in mind that soy milk and soybeans do not naturally contain vitamin B12, so picking a fortified variety of soy milk (and other plant milks) is recommended. Choose unsweetened varieties to keep the amount of added sugars to a minimum.

Pasta from Beans

A fun and nutritious way to add more protein to your diet is by eating pasta—bean pasta, that is! You can now find pasta made from beans and legumes, primarily chickpeas, black beans, and lentils. Loaded with fiber and protein, they can also be a good choice for people who are gluten-intolerant, as they hold their shape much better than pastas made from quinoa or corn. Just 1 ounce (28 g) of dried pasta made from beans contains 5 to 7 grams of protein on average. Bean pasta can have an assertive flavor, so you'll want to top it with a hearty and flavorful sauce. Among the more popular brands of bean pasta are Explore Cuisine, Banza, and Tolerant. Look for them in well-stocked supermarkets and online.

Grains

Seitan

Seitan is a popular protein source made from gluten, the main protein in wheat. Also known as wheat meat or wheat gluten, it contains about 25 grams of protein per 3.5 ounces (99 g). It can be found in the refrigerated section of natural food stores and well-stocked supermarkets. However, I recommend making seitan at home (page 168) since it is easy and economical to prepare and buying ready-to-use seitan can be expensive. Seitan can be pan-fried, sautéed, and even grilled. Because it is made from wheat, seitan should be avoided by people with celiac disease or gluten intolerance.

Oats and Oatmeal

Oats are an easy and delicious way to add protein to any diet. A serving of ½ cup (78 g) of dry old-fashioned oats contains about 6 grams of protein. At 10 grams per ½-cup (88 g) serving, dry steel-cut oats contain even more protein than rolled oats. They also have a lower glycemic index than rolled oats, which means they don't spike blood sugar as much, so you're likely to be more satisfied and experience fewer cravings after eating oatmeal made from steel-cut oats.

Spelt and Teff

Spelt and teff are known as ancient grains. Spelt is a type of wheat and contains gluten, whereas teff is gluten-free. Cooked, spelt offers 11 grams of protein per cup (194 g), while cooked teff offers 10 grams of protein per cup (252 g), making them higher in protein than other ancient grains. Both are excellent sources of various nutrients, including complex carbs, fiber, iron, magnesium, phosphorus, and manganese, as well as B vitamins, zinc, and selenium. Spelt and teff are versatile alternatives to common grains, such as wheat and rice.

Quinoa and Amaranth

Quinoa is a grain with a high protein content and is a complete protein. Cooked quinoa contains 8 grams of protein per cup (185 g). This grain is also rich in other nutrients, including magnesium, iron, fiber, and manganese. Like quinoa, amaranth provides 8 to 9 grams of protein per cooked cup (246 g) and is a source of complete protein. Both quinoa and amaranth are good sources of complex carbs, fiber, iron, manganese, phosphorus, and magnesium

Brown Rice and Wild Rice

Cooked long-grain brown rice contains 5 grams of protein per cup (185 g), whereas the same amount of cooked white rice contains 4.3 grams. Brown rice is also higher in other nutrients than white rice. One cooked cup (165 g) of wild rice provides 7 grams of protein, in addition to a good amount of fiber, manganese, magnesium, copper, phosphorus, and B vitamins.

Sprouted Whole Grain Bread

Compared to more traditional breads, breads made from sprouted whole grains, such as Ezekiel bread, have enhanced protein and nutrient profiles. This nutrient-dense sprouted grain bread is made from barley, wheat, lentils, millet, soy beans, and spelt. It contains 4 grams of protein per slice. You can get even more protein by toasting Ezekiel bread and spreading it with peanut or almond butter.

Nuts

Nuts and seeds (as well as "butters" made from them) are great sources of protein. Depending on the nut and seed variety, 1 ounce (28 g) contains between 3 to 7 grams of protein (or more). In addition to being a great source of protein, nuts are good sources of fiber and a number of vitamins and minerals, including magnesium and vitamin E. Most of the fat in nuts is monounsaturated fat, as well as omega-6 and omega-3 polyunsaturated fat. Nuts have also been shown to reduce risk factors for many chronic diseases, including heart disease and diabetes.

Almonds

With 6 grams of protein in a 1-ounce (28 g) serving, almonds are tree nuts that contain beneficial nutrients believed to improve cholesterol levels, reduce heart disease, and reduce inflammation in people with type 2 diabetes.

Brazil nuts

There are 4 grams of protein in a 1-ounce (28 g) serving. Brazil nuts are the single best source of selenium in the world, an important mineral that acts as an antioxidant.

Cashews

In addition to 5 grams of protein in a 1-ounce (28 g) serving, cashews contain beta-carotene, the antioxidants lutein and zeaxanthin, vitamin E, and oleic acid, which are beneficial for our eyesight and help protect against macular degeneration. Cashew nuts provide a good source of copper, manganese, and magnesium and have been shown to improve blood lipid levels and reduce blood pressure.

Hazelnuts

With 6 grams of protein in a 1-ounce (28 g) serving, hazelnuts are known to improve cholesterol levels and increase the amount of vitamin E in the blood. A significant source of polyphenols that provide powerful antioxidant effects in the body, hazelnuts may also reduce heart disease risk factors.

Peanuts

Technically a legume, peanuts have similar nutrient profiles and health benefits as tree nuts and contain 7 grams of protein in a 1-ounce (28 g) serving. Peanuts have been shown to help reduce risk factors for heart disease and diabetes.

Pecans

Containing 3 grams of protein in a 1-ounce (28 g) serving, pecans are especially rich in polyphenols that act as antioxidants and are known to have lowered "bad" LDL cholesterol in people with normal cholesterol levels.

Pistachios

Rich in omega-6 and omega-3 fatty acids, pistachios contain 6 grams of protein in a 1-ounce (28 g) serving and are also high in fiber. Pistachios may improve cholesterol levels; help reduce other heart disease risk factors, including blood pressure; and help reduce the rise in blood sugar after a meal.

Walnuts

Walnuts contain 4.3 grams of protein in a 1-ounce (28 g) serving as well as a significant amount of phytochemicals and healthy fats. Walnuts are an excellent source of the omega-3 alpha-linolenic acid and seem to have positive effects on brain health and help maintain healthy cognitive function. Walnut consumption decreases blood pressure, lowers blood glucose, and reduces diabetes risk.

Seed Thoughts

When you include seeds in your healthy plant-based diet, you will be getting a good balance of omega-3 and omega-6 fatty acids. These are essential fats that your body can't produce and must obtain from food. These fatty acids play an important role in heart and brain function and studies have shown that people who have a good balance of these fatty acids are less likely to develop chronic disease. The good news is that eating these seeds can be as simple as sprinkling them on top of beans, greens, and salads or mixing them into your morning oatmeal.

Chia seeds

A source of complete protein that contains 2 grams of protein per tablespoon (11 g), chia seeds have the added bonus of soluble fiber, which fills you up quickly and helps slow down the absorption of sugar, making them a good choice for diabetics.

Flaxseeds

An excellent source of omega-3 and omega-6 fatty acids, flaxseeds are especially rich in lignans, which benefit the body in many ways. Flaxseeds are available in both golden and brown varieties. I prefer golden flaxseeds because the color blends in better with other ingredients. I generally grind flaxseeds before using them to make them more digestible.

Hemp seeds

Hemp seeds are a complete protein, with 10 grams of complete, easily digestible protein per ounce (28 g) (that's 5 grams of protein per tablespoon [7 g]). They can be used in a similar way to chia seeds and can be purchased online; look for hulled hemp seeds. Hemp seeds provide more protein than flaxseeds or chia seeds and no other food contains the ideal ratio of omega-3 and omega-6 like hemp seed does.

Pumpkin seed kernels

With 7 grams of protein in a 1-ounce (28 g) serving, just a small amount of pumpkin seeds can provide a good amount of healthy fats, magnesium, and zinc. Pumpkin seeds are rich in antioxidants, iron, zinc, and magnesium and contribute to improved heart health, prostate health, and protection against certain cancers.

Sesame seeds

With 5 grams of protein per 1-ounce (28 g) serving, sesame seeds are a good source of healthy fats, protein, B vitamins, minerals, fiber, and antioxidants. Sesame seeds can also help control blood sugar, combat arthritis pain, and lower cholesterol.

Sunflower seed kernels

Especially high in vitamin E and selenium, sunflower seeds contain 5.5 grams of protein in a 1-ounce (28 g) serving. Sunflower seeds are also rich in antioxidants.

Nut and Seed Butters

High-quality nut butters without added sweeteners or preservatives have nutrient profiles similar to the nuts from which they're made. Two tablespoons (32 g) contain an average of 190 calories and 17 grams of mostly heart-healthy unsaturated fat along with a few grams of protein and some key vitamins and minerals. When choosing any type of nut butter, read the label and check that the nut or seed is the first ingredient—and anything thereafter is natural (or, best of all, there aren't any other added ingredients).

Protein-Rich Vegetables and Fruits

While all vegetables and fruits contain some protein, there are some that contain more protein than others. Vegetables with the most protein include broccoli, spinach, asparagus, artichokes, white potatoes, sweet potatoes, and Brussels sprouts. They contain 4 to 5 grams of protein per cooked cup (235 ml). Fresh fruits generally have a lower protein content than vegetables. Those containing the most include guava, blackberries, nectarines, and bananas, which have 2 to 4 grams of protein per cup (235 ml).

What about Other Nutrients?

While this book is focused on plant protein, please be aware that plant foods are also loaded with other great nutrients.

For example, in addition to being protein rich, beans contain lots of fiber, B vitamins, magnesium, and many other vitamins and minerals. Soy foods are also high in iron, vitamin K, and phosphorus. Spinach is high in vitamins A and K and is loaded with antioxidants. Carrots are full of beta carotene and vitamin C. Just 1 cup (71 g) of broccoli provides 135 percent of your vitamin C requirements. And these are just a few examples. But no one ever asks you if you're getting enough vitamin C or A, do they? The question is always "Are you getting enough protein?" When you eat the high-protein plant-based recipes in this book, you can answer with a resounding "yes."

Vegan Diet vs. Plant-Based Diet vs. Whole-Food, Plant-Based Diet

A **vegan diet** eliminates all animal products of all kinds, 100 percent of the time, often predominantly for ethical reasons.

With a **plant-based diet**, the majority of food comes from plants and is usually motivated by reasons of health. Some people who follow a plant-based diet do include small amounts of animal products.

A **whole-food, plant-based diet** consists of whole plant foods and avoids highly refined foods such as bleached flour, refined sugar, and most oil.

It is possible (and common) to be both vegan and plant-based or whole-food, plant-based.

Protein Amounts in Plant Foods

This is a listing of plant foods with significant amounts of protein.

Beans and Legumes

- Black beans, cooked, 1 cup (172 g) = 15.2 grams protein

- Chickpea flour, 1 cup (85 g) = 21 grams protein

- Chickpeas, cooked, 1 cup (164 g) = 14.5 grams protein

- Kidney beans, cooked, 1 cup (177 g) = 13.4 grams protein

- Lentils, cooked, 1 cup (198 g) = 18 grams protein

- Navy beans, cooked, 1 cup (182 g) = 15.0 grams protein

- Green peas, cooked, 1 cup (130 g) = 8 grams protein

- Pinto beans, cooked, 1 cup (171 g) = 15.4 grams protein

Soy Foods

- Edamame, shelled and cooked, 1 cup (235 ml) = 17 grams protein

- Soybeans, cooked, 1 cup (235 ml) = 28.6 grams protein

- Tempeh, ½ cup diced (120 ml) = 15 grams protein

- Tofu, 1 cup diced (235 ml) = 20 grams protein

- Soy milk, 1 cup (235 ml) = 7 grams protein

Grains

- Amaranth, cooked, 1 cup (246 g) = 9 grams protein

- Brown rice, cooked, 1 cup (185 g) = 5 grams protein

- Buckwheat, cooked, 1 cup (120 g) = 6 grams protein

- Bulgur, cooked, 1 cup (150 g) = 6 grams protein

- Oats, cooked, 1 cup (234 g) = 6 grams protein

- Quinoa, cooked, 1 cup (185 g) = 8 grams protein

- Seitan (wheat gluten), 3 ounces (85 g) = 21 grams protein

- Spelt, cooked, 1 cup (194 g) = 11 grams protein

- Teff, cooked, 1 cup (252 g) = 10 grams protein

Nuts and Seeds

- Almonds, ¼ cup (36 g) = 6 grams protein

- Peanuts, ¼ cup (35 g) = 5 grams protein

- Cashews, ¼ cup (34 g) = 5.2 grams protein

- Chia seeds, 2 tablespoons (22 g) = 4 grams protein

- Flaxseeds, golden, 2 tablespoons (24 g) = 4 grams protein

- Hemp seeds, hulled, 2 tablespoons (14 g) = 6.6 grams protein

- Pecans, ¼ cup (28 g) = 3 grams protein

- Pistachios, ¼ cup (31 g) = 6 grams protein

- Pumpkin seed kernels (pepitas), ½ cup (114 g) = 6 grams protein

- Sesame seeds, ¼ cup (32 g) = 6.5 grams protein

- Sunflower seeds kernels, ¼ cup (36 g) = 5.5 grams protein

- Walnuts, ¼ cup (25 g) = 4.3 grams protein

Nut and Seed Butters

- Almond butter, 2 tablespoons (32 g) = 6.8 grams protein

- Peanut butter, 2 tablespoons (32 g) = 8 grams protein

- Soy nut butter, 2 tablespoons (32 g) = 7 grams protein

- Iahini, 2 tablespoons = (30 g) 5.2 grams protein

Plant Milks

- Almond milk, 1 cup (235 ml) = 2 grams protein

- Cashew milk, 1 cup (235 ml) = 2 grams protein

- Hemp milk, 1 cup (235 ml) = 4.7 grams protein

- Oat milk, 1 cup (235 ml) = 3 grams protein

- Pea protein milk, 1 cup (235 ml) = 8 grams protein

- Soy milk, 1 cup (235 ml) = 8 grams protein

Vegetables

- Artichoke, 1 medium = 3.4 grams protein

- Asparagus, 6 spears = 2.1 grams protein

- Avocado, 1 medium = 4.2 grams protein

- Bok choy, 1 cup (70 g) sliced = 2.6 grams protein

- Broccoli, 1 medium stalk = 4 grams protein

- Brussels sprouts, 1 cup (88 g) = 3.9 grams protein

- Cauliflower, 1 cup (124 g) cooked = 2.2 grams protein

- Kale, 1 packed cup (130 g) cooked = 2.5 grams protein

- Mushrooms, 5 medium: 3 grams protein

- Peas, green, 1 cup (130 g) cooked = 9 grams protein

- Spinach, 1 packed cup (180 g) cooked = 6 grams protein

- Sweet potato, 1 medium = 2.2 grams protein

- White potato, 1 large = 8 grams protein

- Yellow corn, 1 large ear = 4.6 grams protein

- Zucchini, 1 medium = 2.4 grams protein

Miscellaneous

- Nutritional yeast, 2 tablespoons (8 g) = 4 grams protein (get one fortified with vitamin B12)

- Sprouted grain bread, 1 slice = 4 grams protein

- Sprouted grain tortilla, 1 tortilla = 6 grams protein

- Spirulina (blue-green algae), 2 tablespoons (30 ml) = 8 grams protein

- Vegan protein powder blends, 1 scoop = 15 to 20 grams protein

Super Eight

Here are eight great (and easy) ways to get 15 grams (or more) of plant protein in one tasty serving, morning, noon, and night.

Breakfast

1. Spread 2 tablespoons (32 g) of nut butter (any kind) and 1 tablespoon (7 g) hulled hemp seeds on 1 slice of toasted sprouted grain bread.

2. Eat a bowl of oatmeal made with ½ cup (88 g) steel-cut oats, 1 tablespoon (11 g) chia seeds, 2 tablespoons (32 g) almond butter, and a splash of soy milk.

3. Add 2 tablespoons (32 g) nut butter (any kind), 1 tablespoon (11 g) chia seeds or ground hemp seeds, and ½ cup (120 ml) soy milk or silken tofu to your smoothie.

Lunch

4. Add 1 cup (164 g) cooked chickpeas to your salad and sprinkle the salad with 2 tablespoons (24 g) ground golden flaxseeds or 2 tablespoons (14 g) hulled hemp seeds.

5. Top a large baked potato with 2 tablespoons (32 g) almond butter and 1 tablespoon (4 g) nutritional yeast.

Dinner

6. Combine 1 cup (155 g) cooked edamame and 1 cup (164 g) cooked corn kernels for a protein-rich succotash.

7. Sauté 2 cups (60 g) spinach with 1 cup (177 g) of cooked white beans and season with Protein Parm (page 129).

8. Sprinkle 1 tablespoon (4 g) nutritional yeast on 1 cup (185 g) cooked quinoa and ½ cup (86 g) cooked black beans.

A Word about Processed Products

Plant-based meat products such as burgers, sausage, and nuggets seem to be everywhere these days, even in mainstream fast-food chains. Personally, I think that's a good thing, because more people eating foods made from plants means that fewer animals are being eaten.

However, the fact remains that many of these plant-based products are highly processed and may be high in fat as well. So while they may be a tasty once-in-a-while treat, the best approach for your health in the long-term is to strive to adopt a whole-foods, plant-based diet that will not only provide you with ample protein, but also give you all the other nutrients you need.

For those would like to enjoy the flavors of such foods without the baggage of excessive amounts of oil, sodium, and other ingredients found in highly processed products, I've included healthier recipes for plant-based sausage, ham, mayonnaise, and other similar foods.

What about Protein Powders?

Many people, especially those with an active and/or busy lifestyle, enjoy using protein powder supplements as an easy and convenient way to add an extra boost of protein to their daily food intake. These products can certainly pack a healthy protein punch when added to a smoothie or mixed into oatmeal. If you like the idea of a quick way to up your protein intake, look for a vegan protein powder blend made from raw sprouted whole grains. Just remember to use the protein powder as a supplement to your protein intake rather than relying on it as a main source of protein.

About the Recipes in This Book

The recipes in this book are 100 percent vegan as well as plant-based, and many are whole-food, plant based or have whole-food, plant-based options.

These recipes were developed to give you delicious, easy-to-prepare, family-friendly meals that also maximize your plant protein intake. The recipe chapters are organized according to the type of meal, such as appetizers, soups, salads, oven-baked dinners, and breakfast. There's even a chapter devoted to protein-rich desserts. The final chapter features recipes for protein-rich, plant-based alternatives to meat and dairy foods that are used in a variety of ways throughout the book.

Most of the recipes in this book are free of refined flours and processed ingredients. Many of them use little or no oil, or have an oil-free option. In my own home, I use very little oil, preferring to water-sauté, roast, or air-fry whenever possible. The main reason oil is called for as a first choice in some of the recipes is when it adds a particular nuance to a dish, such as browning or crisping. Still, if you choose to eliminate all oil from your diet, feel free to eliminate it from those recipes as well, substituting water or broth, as needed.

If you don't find an alternative listed for something you are allergic to or prefer not to eat, feel free to customize the recipes to suit your needs or preferences as described in the Food Allergies section on page 10.

Adding More Protein to the Recipes

The recipes in this book are designed to pack a healthy protein punch, but there are ways to add even more protein to them, if you choose to do so. Here are five easy ways to add more protein to the recipes:

1. Use bean pasta in place of regular pasta in the pasta recipes.

2. Add extra beans, quinoa, or tofu to stews, stir-fries, and casseroles.

3. Use plain unsweetened soy milk in recipes calling for plant milk.

4. Sprinkle hulled hemp seeds on top of salads, pasta, and grain dishes.

5. Add a scoop of vegan protein powder to smoothies, oatmeal, and baked goods.

Chapter 2
Appetizers and Snacks

Hummus
Among Us

1½ cups (246 g) cooked chickpeas, or 1 (15-ounce [425 g]) can, rinsed and drained

2 garlic cloves, coarsely chopped

2 tablespoons (30 ml) cold water, plus more if needed

⅓ cup (80 g) tahini

2 tablespoons (30 ml) fresh lemon juice

½ teaspoon sea salt, plus more if needed

1 tablespoon (15 ml) Everything Seasoning Mix (page 38), to garnish (optional)

Hummus is an ever-present fixture at plant-based get-togethers, and with good reason. It's delicious, easy to make, and goes well with crackers, cut veggies, and chips. It also makes a good sandwich spread. A sprinkling of Everything Seasoning Mix (page 38) adds flavor and protein. If you're a garlic lover, you can add an extra clove or two of garlic, but keep in mind that the Everything Seasoning adds more garlic flavor as well.

1. Combine the chickpeas, garlic, and water in a food processor. Process to a fine paste. Add the tahini, lemon juice, and salt. Process the hummus until completely smooth, stopping to scrape down the sides of the food processor as need. If the hummus is too thick, add another tablespoon of water. Taste and adjust the seasonings, adding more salt if needed.

2. Transfer the hummus to a small serving bowl and sprinkle the top with the Everything Seasoning, if using. Serve or store in an airtight container in the refrigerator for up to 3 days.

Nutrition Analysis

Per serving: 150 calories, 6 g protein, 8 g total fat, 15 g carbohydrate, 2 g sugar, 4 g fiber

Edamame Guacamole

½ cup (76 g) edamame, cooked until very soft, then drained and cooled

2 ripe Hass avocados, peeled and pitted

1 tablespoon (15 ml) fresh lime juice

¼ teaspoon sea salt

⅛ teaspoon ground cumin

¼ cup (60 ml) canned chopped green chiles or mild or hot salsa

1 tablespoon (4 g) minced fresh cilantro (optional)

Whole-grain tortilla chips or raw veggies, to serve

Using protein-rich edamame to replace some of the avocado makes this dip higher in protein than your standard guacamole. Frozen shelled edamame is the most convenient way to buy them for this recipe. Be sure to cook the edamame until very soft so that they puree well in the food processor. If you are allergic to soy, you can substitute frozen green peas for the edamame.

1. Process the edamame in a food processor until smooth. Scoop the avocado into the food processor, then add the lime juice, salt, and cumin. If you like a smoother guacamole, process until smooth; if you prefer a chunkier texture, pulse to combine.

2. Transfer to a serving bowl and stir in the chiles or salsa. Sprinkle the top with cilantro, if using. Serve with tortilla chips or raw vegetables.

Nutrition Analysis

Per serving [for 4]: 140 calories, 3 g protein, 11 g total fat, 9 g carbohydrate, 1 g sugar, 6 g fiber

Per serving [for 6]: 90 calories, 2 g protein, 8 g total fat, 6 g carbohydrate, 0 g sugar, 4 g fiber

Everything Cheesy Wheel

1½ cups (45 g) raw cashews, soaked in hot water for 30 minutes, well drained

⅓ cup (21 g) nutritional yeast

2 tablespoon (30 ml) fresh lemon juice

1½ teaspoons white miso paste

½ teaspoon onion powder

¼ teaspoon garlic powder

¼ teaspoon sea salt

⅓ cup (40 g) Everything Seasoning Mix (page 38)

This easy cheesy wheel gets its name from the seasoning mix it's coated with. If you prefer a different coating, try ground walnuts or minced chives. Serve with whole-grain crackers.

1. Line a 4-inch (10 cm) springform pan or a 2-cup (475 ml) ramekin with cheesecloth, draping the ends over the edge. Set aside.

2. In a food processor, combine the cashews, nutritional yeast, lemon juice, miso, onion powder, garlic powder, and salt. Pulse until smooth, scraping down the sides as needed. Scoop the mixture into the prepared pan and bring up the sides of the cheesecloth to cover the top of the cheese mixture. Press down on the cheese mixture to spread it evenly in the pan and flatten the top. Refrigerate for 3 hours, then remove from the refrigerator, and remove from the container.

3. Remove the cheesecloth and dredge the cheese wheel in the seasoning mix until covered, pressing the coating into the cheese. Transfer the coated cheese wheel to a plate, cover, and refrigerate until ready to serve.

Nutrition Analysis

Per serving [for 6]: 90 calories, 4 g protein, 5 g total fat, 8 g carbohydrate, 1 g sugar, 2 g fiber

Per serving [for 8]: 65 calories, 3 g protein, 4 g total fat, 6 g carbohydrate, 1 g sugar, 2 g fiber

Everything Seasoning Mix

Makes about ³/₄ cup (91 g)

2 tablespoons (16 g) white sesame seeds

1 tablespoon (8 g) black sesame seeds

2 tablespoons (7 g) dried minced onion flakes

1½ tablespoons (15 g) dried minced garlic

3 tablespoons (33 g) chia seeds

3 tablespoons (3 g) coarse sea salt

1 tablespoon (9 g) poppy seeds

This everything mix is not just for bagels. Use it to coat the Everything Cheese Wheel (page 36) or sprinkle it on baked potatoes, avocado toast, salads, and more. My version contains chia seeds in addition to the traditional poppy seeds for an extra boost of protein.

1. In a small skillet, combine the white and black sesame seeds, onion flakes, and garlic and heat over medium heat, stirring constantly, until fragrant and lightly browned, 1 to 2 minutes. Do not burn.

2. Transfer to a heatproof bowl and stir in the chia seeds, salt, and poppy seeds. Mix together until well combined. Let cool completely before using. The seasoning mix can be stored in an airtight container at room temperature for up to 1 month.

Nutrition Analysis

Per 1-tablespoon (7 g) serving: 35 calories, 1 g protein, 2 g total fat, 3 g carbohydrate, 1 g sugar, 1 g fiber

Sunflower-Crusted Cashew Cheddar

Makes 6 to 8 servings

1⅓ cups (39 g) raw cashews, soaked in hot water for 15 minutes, then well-drained

2 tablespoons (22 g) chopped roasted red pepper, drained and blotted dry

1 tablespoon (15 ml) rice vinegar

1 tablespoon (15 ml) beer (optional)

2 teaspoons white miso paste

½ teaspoon Dijon mustard

¼ cup (16 g) nutritional yeast

1 teaspoon onion powder

¾ teaspoon sea salt

½ teaspoon smoked paprika

¼ teaspoon ground turmeric

1 cup (235 ml) coarsely ground sunflower seed kernels

This easy-to-make cheddar blend gets its ample protein from cashews and sunflower seeds. Use a high-speed blender, such as a Vitamix or BlendTec, for the best result. You can also make this in a food processor, but the cheese won't be as smooth. Serve with your favorite whole-grain crackers.

1. In a high-speed blender, combine the cashews, red pepper, vinegar, beer, if using, miso, and mustard. Process until the mixture is a smooth paste. Add the nutritional yeast, onion powder, salt, paprika, and turmeric. Process until smooth, scraping down the sides as needed.

2. Transfer the mixture to a small colander lined with cheesecloth. Fold the cheesecloth over top of the cheese mixture and place the colander in a bowl to catch any liquid. Refrigerate overnight.

3. Unwrap the cheese and use your hands to shape it into a smooth ball or log. Roll the cheese into the ground sunflower seeds, pressing lightly to make them adhere. Transfer the cheese to a plate and refrigerate until ready to serve.

Nutrition Analysis

Per serving [for 6]: 101 calories, 8 g protein, 5 g total fat, 9 g carbohydrate, 2 g sugar, 3 g fiber

Per serving [for 8]: 73 calories, 6 g protein, 4 g total fat, 7 g carbohydrate, 1 g sugar, 2 g fiber

Faux Gras

2 tablespoons (30 ml) water, or 1 tablespoon (15 ml) extra-virgin olive oil

1 small yellow onion, chopped

2 garlic cloves, minced

1 cup (70 g) sliced cremini mushrooms

2 cups (396 g) cooked green lentils, well drained and blotted dry

1 cup (100 g) toasted walnuts or pecans

1½ tablespoons (23 ml) fresh lemon juice

1 tablespoon (15 ml) tamari

1½ teaspoons dried thyme

½ teaspoon ground coriander

½ teaspoon dried sage

1 tablespoon (4 g) minced fresh parsley

1 tablespoon (15 ml) brandy

1 teaspoon natural sugar

Sea salt and freshly ground black pepper

Toasted sliced baguette rounds or crackers, to serve

This delectable spread is packed with flavor and protein. Plan to make it a day before serving to allow the flavor to intensify. This recipe makes a lot (about 4 cups [946 ml]), but it freezes well. It's also fantastic to use on the banh mi sandwiches on page 82 in place of the tofu.

1. Heat the water in a skillet over medium heat. Add the onion and garlic, and cook, stirring frequently, until the onion is softened, about 5 minutes. Add the mushrooms and cook, stirring occasionally, until soft, about 5 minutes longer. Remove from the heat.

2. In a food processor, combine the cooked lentils, walnuts, lemon juice, tamari, thyme, coriander, sage, parsley, brandy, sugar, and salt and pepper to taste. Add the cooked mushroom mixture and process until completely smooth. Taste and adjust the seasonings, if needed. Transfer the mixture to a serving bowl and smooth the top. Refrigerate for about 3 hours to firm up.

3. Serve with toasted sliced baguette rounds or crackers. Cover leftovers tightly and refrigerate for up to 4 days, or freeze for up to 3 months.

Nutrition Analysis

Per serving [for 6]: 200 calories, 9 g protein, 11 g total fat, 18 g carbohydrate, 3 g sugar, 7 g fiber

Per serving [for 8]: 150 calories, 7 g protein, 8 g total fat, 14 g carbohydrate, 2 g sugar, 5 g fiber

Two-Bean Nachos

Makes 4 to 6 servings

1¾ cups Easy Cheesy Sauce (recipe follows), kept warm

1 (12-ounce [340 g]) bag whole-grain tortilla chips

1½ cups (355 g) cooked black beans, or 1 (15-ounce [425 g]) can, rinsed and drained

1½ cups (354 g) cooked dark red kidney beans, or 1 (15-ounce [425 g]) can, rinsed and drained

1 large ripe tomato, diced

½ cup (80 g) chopped red onion or scallions, white and green parts

¼ cup (60 ml) chopped pickled jalapeños

¼ cup (15 g) chopped fresh cilantro (optional)

2 tablespoons (14 g) hulled hemp seeds

1 ripe Hass avocado, peeled, pitted, and diced

1 tablespoon (15 ml) fresh lime juice

Sea salt

Nachos are a fun food to serve at casual get-togethers. Make the cheesy sauce in advance and the nachos will come together quickly.

1. Prepare the sauce and keep it warm. Preheat the oven to 350°F (180°C).

2. Spread the tortilla chips in a single layer on a large rimmed baking sheet and bake until the chips are crisp and warm, about 5 minutes.

3. Remove the baking sheet from the oven. Sprinkle the black beans evenly over the chips, followed by the red kidney beans, tomato, onion, jalapeños, cilantro, if using, and the hemp seeds. In a small bowl, toss the avocado with the lime juice and season with salt. Top the nachos with the avocado, then drizzle the warmed cheesy sauce over the nachos and serve immediately.

Nutrition Analysis

Per serving: 550 calories, 17 g protein, 23 g total fat, 68 g carbohydrate, 5 g sugar, 10 g fiber

Easy Cheesy Sauce

Makes 8 servings

1¼ cups (38 g) raw cashews, soaked in hot water for 30 minutes, then well-drained

⅓ cup (21 g) nutritional yeast

2 tablespoons (30 ml) jarred roasted red pepper, drained and blotted dry

1 tablespoon (15 ml) rice vinegar

1 tablespoon (15 ml) fresh lemon juice

2 teaspoons white miso paste

1 teaspoon sea salt

½ teaspoon smoked paprika

½ teaspoon onion powder

½ teaspoon prepared yellow mustard

¼ teaspoon ground turmeric

1 cup (235 ml) plain unsweetened plant milk, plus more as needed

This creamy golden sauce is rich and full of flavorful protein-rich goodness. I use it to drizzle over nachos and as a topping for baked potatoes, roasted vegetables, and enchiladas.

1. Combine all the ingredients in a high-speed blender. Process until the mixture is pureed and smooth, scraping down the sides, as needed. The sauce is now ready to use in recipes.

2. Use as is, or heat gently in a saucepan for a minute or two, stirring in a little more milk, if needed, for a thinner sauce.

Variation:

Make it into a queso dip. Simply add some pickled chopped jalapenos and chili powder, and cut back on the plant milk by one-third to one-half, then heat until warm and serve with tortilla chips.

Nutrition Analysis

Per ¼-cup (60 ml) serving: 50 calories, 3 g protein, 3 g total fat, 4 g carbohydrate, 1 g sugar, 1 g fiber

Country-Style Lentil Pâté

2 tablespoons (30 ml) water, or 1 tablespoon (15 ml) extra-virgin olive oil

1 large yellow onion, chopped

2 garlic cloves, minced

3 cups (594 g) cooked brown lentils, well drained and blotted dry

1 teaspoon dried marjoram

1 teaspoon dried thyme

2 tablespoons (30 ml) tamari

2 tablespoons (30 ml) brandy

1 tablespoon (16 g) tomato paste

1 tablespoon (16 g) white miso paste

1 cup (100 g) toasted walnuts or pecans

½ cup (73 g) sunflower seed kernels

½ cup (43 g) chickpea flour

¼ cup (16 g) nutritional yeast

½ teaspoon sea salt

¼ teaspoon freshly ground black pepper

2 tablespoons (14 g) ground golden flaxseeds, combined with 2 tablespoons (30 ml) warm water

The hearty pâté makes a great appetizer spread onto celery sticks, toast, crackers, or pita crisps. It's also a delicious sandwich filling.

1. Preheat the oven to 350°F (180°C). Lightly oil a 6-cup (1.5 L) loaf pan or pâté mold with parchment paper cut to fit or spray it with cooking spray.

2. Heat the water in a large skillet over medium heat. Add the onion and cook until softened, about 5 minutes. Add the garlic and cook, stirring, for 3 minutes. Stir in the lentils, marjoram, thyme, tamari, brandy, tomato paste, and miso paste. Stir to mix well. Cook until all the liquid evaporates, 2 to 3 minutes. Remove from the heat and set aside.

3. In a food processor, grind the walnuts and sunflower seeds until coarsely ground. Add the chickpea flour, nutritional yeast, salt, and pepper. Process until well combined. Add the lentil mixture and the flaxseed mixture. Pulse until the mixture is combined but not pureed, leaving some texture. Taste and adjust the seasonings, if needed.

4. Spoon the mixture into the prepared pan and smooth the top evenly. Spray or brush the top of with olive oil, then cover the pan tightly with aluminum foil and place the pan inside a large baking dish with about an inch (2.5 cm) of hot water in the bottom. Bake until firm, about 1 hour. Let the pâté cool in the pan, then refrigerate until well chilled for easier slicing.

5. To serve, carefully loosen the edges of the pâté with a knife, if necessary, and invert onto a serving platter. Serve at room temperature. Store leftovers in the refrigerator, tightly wrapped for up to 5 days, or frozen for up to 3 months.

Nutrition Analysis

Per serving: 280 calories, 14 g protein, 14 g total fat, 26 g carbohydrate, 4 g sugar, 9 g fiber

Little Lentil Balls

Makes 6 servings (About 36
(1-inch [2.5 cm]) lentil balls

1 tablespoon (7 g) ground golden flaxseeds, combined with 2 tablespoons (30 ml) hot water

2 garlic cloves, crushed or coarsely chopped

1 cup (70 g) coarsely chopped mushrooms (any type)

2 tablespoons (30 ml) water, or 1 tablespoon (15 ml) extra-virgin olive oil

1½ cups (275 g) cooked brown lentils, well drained and blotted dry

1 tablespoon (16 g) tomato paste

2 tablespoons (18 g) vital wheat gluten

½ cup (78 g) quick-cooking oats, plus more if needed

2 tablespoons (8 g) nutritional yeast

2 tablespoons (8 g) minced fresh parsley

1 teaspoon dried basil

½ teaspoon smoked paprika

½ teaspoon sea salt

¼ teaspoon freshly ground black pepper

Dried bread crumbs (optional)

Water (optional)

Marinara sauce or other sauce, warmed, for dipping

Nutrition Analysis

Per serving: 120 calories, 9 g protein, 1 g total fat, 18 g carbohydrate, 2 g sugar, 6 g fiber

These meaty little balls may be small in size, but they're big in flavor. Serve them as an appetizer with marinara sauce, a tangy barbecue sauce, or a sweet and sour sauce. If you make them larger like traditional meatballs, you can serve them with pasta and marinara sauce or use them to make a sandwich or sub with tomato sauce and vegan cheese. These balls freeze well, so make extra to have them on hand.

1. In a food processor, process the garlic until finely minced. Add the mushrooms and pulse until finely chopped, but not pureed.

2. Heat the water in a skillet over medium heat. Add the mushroom mixture and cook for a few minutes, stirring until the mushrooms release their liquid and the liquid evaporates. Stir in the lentils and tomato paste, then remove from the heat and transfer to a mixing bowl. Add the vital wheat gluten, oats, nutritional yeast, parsley, flaxseed mixture, basil, paprika, salt, and pepper. Mix well and set aside to cool for a few minutes.

3. Meanwhile, preheat the oven to 400°F (200°C). Line a large rimmed baking sheet with parchment paper or coat with cooking spray.

4. When the mixture is cool enough to handle, use your hands to press the mixture together. It should hold together well. If it's too wet, add some dried bread crumbs or more oats, 1 tablespoon (15 ml) at a time. If it's too dry, add a little water, 1 tablespoon at a time.

5. Pinch off a small piece of the mixture, press it together in your hand, and then roll between your palms to make a 1- to 1½-inch (2.5 to 3.5 cm) ball. Repeat until the mixture is used up, arranging the balls in rows on the prepared baking sheet.

6. Bake for about 18 minutes, or until firm and nicely browned, turning once about halfway through. Serve with a bowl of warm marinara sauce for dipping.

Roasted Smoky Chickpeas

Makes 4 to 6 servings

2 tablespoons (30 ml) tamari

1 tablespoon (20 g) pure maple syrup

1 tablespoon (15 ml) extra-virgin olive oil

1 teaspoon liquid smoke

¼ teaspoon smoked paprika

1½ cups (246 g) cooked chickpeas, or 1 (15-ounce [425 g]) can, rinsed and drained

After spending time in a smoky marinade, chickpeas become firm and crunchy when roasted. They make a great high-protein snack or topping for salads and grain or noodle dishes, or as a filling ingredient for wrap sandwiches.

1. Preheat the oven to 400°F (200°C). Line a rimmed baking sheet with parchment paper or a light coating of cooking spray.

2. In a bowl, combine the tamari, maple syrup, olive oil, liquid smoke, and paprika. Blot the chickpeas dry and add them to the bowl. Toss gently to coat.

3. Spread the chickpeas evenly in a single layer onto the baking sheet. Bake for about 30 minutes, stirring the chickpeas every 10 minutes to allow them to cook evenly and prevent burning. The chickpeas should be nicely browned.

4. Remove from the oven and serve warm or at room temperature. These are best eaten right away for the best texture.

Air Fryer Variation:

If you have an air fryer, you can get crunchy roasted chickpeas by cooking them in the air fryer for about 15 minutes at 400°F (200°C), shaking the basket every few minutes.

Nutrition Analysis

Per serving [for 4]: 150 calories, 6 g protein, 5 g total fat, 21 g carbohydrate, 6 g sugar, 5 g fiber

Per serving [for 6]: 100 calories, 4 g protein, 3.5 g total fat, 14 g carbohydrate, 4 g sugar, 3 g fiber

Baked Tofu with Peanut Sauce

Makes 4 servings

Peanut Sauce

½ cup (130 g) creamy natural peanut butter

2 tablespoons (30 ml) tamari

2 tablespoons (30 ml) rice vinegar

1½ teaspoons grated fresh ginger

1 teaspoon Asian chili-garlic sauce

1 teaspoon natural sugar

½ cup (120 ml) water

Baked Tofu

12 to 16 ounces (340 to 455 g) extra-firm or super-firm tofu, drained

2 tablespoons (30 ml) tamari

1 tablespoon (8 g) cornstarch

½ teaspoon onion powder

½ teaspoon garlic powder

¼ teaspoon sea salt

This hearty appetizer also makes a great main dish served over rice or tossed with cooked noodles and vegetables. Use an extra-firm (or super-firm, if you can find it) tofu that has been packed in water in a plastic tub.

1. To make the peanut sauce, in a bowl or food processor, combine the peanut butter, tamari, vinegar, ginger, chili-garlic sauce, and sugar. Mix or process well. Slowly add the water, stirring, to make a thick sauce. Taste and adjust the seasonings. Set aside. (When you are ready to serve, warm the sauce in a small saucepan or in the microwave.)

2. To make the tofu, preheat the oven to 400°F (200°C). Line a rimmed baking sheet with parchment paper or coat with cooking spray.

(Continued)

(Continued)

3. Cut the drained tofu block into ¾-inch (2 cm) slabs, then cut the slabs into ¾-inch (2 cm) cubes. Place a clean kitchen towel or a few thicknesses of paper towel on a work surface. Arrange the tofu in a single layer on the towel. Put another clean kitchen towel on top and pat well to remove any moisture. This will help the tofu brown and become crispy.

4. Transfer the tofu cubes to a bowl and add the tamari, stirring gently to combine and coat the tofu. In a small bowl, combine the cornstarch, onion powder, garlic powder, and salt. Mix well. Sprinkle the cornstarch mixture onto the tofu and toss to coat evenly. Arrange the coated tofu in a single layer on the prepared baking sheet. Coat the tofu lightly with cooking spray.

5. Bake the tofu until browned and crisp, 30 to 40 minutes, flipping halfway through.

6. To serve, transfer the tofu to a plate and serve with a bowl of the warm peanut sauce for dipping.

Nutrition Analysis

Per serving (with 12 ounces [340 g] tofu): 320 calories, 18 g protein, 20 g total fat, 13 g carbohydrate, 3 g sugar, 2 g fiber

Per serving (with 16 ounces [455 g] tofu): 350 calories, 20 g protein, 22 g total fat, 14 g carbohydrate, 3 g sugar, 2 g fiber

Sweet and Spicy Nuts

1 cup (100 g) whole walnut halves

1 cup (145 g) whole almonds

1 cup (137 g) whole dry-roasted unsalted cashews

½ cup (50 g) pecan halves

½ cup (75 g) unsalted dry-roasted peanuts

¼ cup (40 g) raw pumpkin seed kernels (pepitas)

½ cup (160 g) pure maple syrup

1 tablespoon (15 ml) neutral-tasting vegetable oil, such as avocado oil

1 teaspoon smoked paprika

¾ teaspoon ground coriander

½ teaspoon ground cumin

¼ teaspoon cayenne

1 teaspoon sea salt

Nuts are the original high-protein snack. While they're certainly delicious unadorned, roasting them in this sweet and spicy mixture really takes them to the next level. Feel free to mix and match the types of nuts you use according to your personal preference.

1. Preheat the oven to 350°F (180°C). Line a rimmed baking sheet with parchment paper or lightly coat it with cooking spray.

2. In a large bowl, combine the walnuts, almonds, cashews, pecans, peanuts, pumpkin seeds, maple syrup, oil, paprika, coriander, cumin, cayenne, and salt. Toss to coat the nuts evenly.

   Transfer the nuts to the prepared pan and spread them in an even layer, separating the nuts with a fork.

3. Roast the nuts for 20 minutes, stirring occasionally, or until they are nicely glazed and golden brown.

4. Remove from the oven and set aside to cool, stirring to break up any clusters. Allow the nuts to cool completely at room temperature before serving. Once the nuts are cool, break up any remaining clusters of nuts. The cooled nuts can be stored in an airtight container at room temperature for up to 2 weeks.

Nutrition Analysis

Per ¼-cup (36 g) serving: 210 calories, 6 g protein, 17 g total fat, 13 g carbohydrate, 7 g sugar, 2 g fiber

Chapter 3
Salad Power

PROTEIN PLUS

Caesar Chef's Salad

Makes 2 to 4 servings

Salad

8 cups (360 g) chopped romaine lettuce

1 carrot, shredded

1½ cups (246 g) cooked chickpeas, or 1 (15-ounce [425 g]) can, rinsed and drained

1 cup (235 ml) diced Baked Marinated Tofu (page 176) or store-bought baked tofu

1 cup (235 ml) diced Ham I Am (page 174) or store-bought vegan ham

1 avocado, peeled, pitted, and diced

1 cup (150 g) grape or cherry tomatoes, quartered lengthwise

¼ cup (36 g) sunflower seed kernels

Creamy Caesar Dressing

⅓ cup (10 g) raw cashew pieces, soaked in hot water for 30 minutes and drained

2 or 3 garlic cloves, crushed or coarsely chopped

½ teaspoon sea salt

2 tablespoons (8 g) nutritional yeast

2 tablespoons (30 ml) fresh lemon juice

1 tablespoon (15 ml) apple cider vinegar

1 tablespoon (16 g) almond butter

1 tablespoon (16 g) white miso paste

2 teaspoons tamari

1½ teaspoons capers

1 teaspoon Dijon mustard

¼ teaspoon freshly ground black pepper

½ cup (235 ml) plain unsweetened plant milk

This protein-rich chef's salad features baked marinated tofu, vegan ham, chickpeas, and sunflower seeds, crowned with a zesty Caesar dressing for even more protein and flavor. It makes two meal-size salads or four side salads.

1. To make the salad, divide the lettuce, carrot, and chickpeas between two or among four salad bowls. Arrange the tofu, ham, and avocado into separate piles on top of each salad. Place the tomato pieces between the tofu, ham, and avocado, and sprinkle the salads with sunflower seeds.

2. To make the dressing, in a high-speed blender, combine all the dressing ingredients. Blend until smooth and creamy. Taste and adjust the seasonings, if needed.

3. Serve the dressing on the side of the salads so people can add as desired.

Nutrition Analysis

Per serving [for 2]: 790 calories, 54 g protein, 30 g total fat, 83 g carbohydrate, 25 g sugar, 23 g fiber

Per serving [for 4]: 410 calories, 28 g protein, 16 g total fat, 43 g carbohydrate, 13 g sugar, 12 g fiber

PROTEIN PLUS

Black Bean Taco Salad

Makes 4 servings

3 cups (516 g) cooked black beans, or 2 (15-ounce [425 g]) cans, rinsed and drained

3 cups (705 ml) tomato-based salsa (mild or hot)

¼ cup (15 g) chopped fresh cilantro

¼ cup (25 g) chopped scallions, white and green parts

1 tablespoon (4 g) nutritional yeast

1 tablespoon (8 g) chili powder

1 teaspoon dried oregano

1 tablespoon (15 ml) tamari

½ teaspoon sea salt

¼ teaspoon freshly ground black pepper

8 cups (376 g) coarsely chopped romaine lettuce

2 plum tomatoes, cut into ¼-inch (6 mm) dice

1 cup (164 g) fresh or frozen corn kernels, steamed

1 avocado, peeled, pitted, and chopped

½ cup (235 ml) Cashew Sour Cream (page 180)

2 cups (53 g) tortilla chips, plus more to serve

This tasty taco salad combines black beans with salsa and seasonings over romaine lettuce and tops it off with tomatoes, corn, avocado, and vegan sour cream, served with crunchy tortilla chips.

1. In a small saucepan, combine the black beans with 2 cups (475 ml) of the salsa. Stir in the cilantro, scallions, nutritional yeast, chili powder, oregano, tamari, salt, pepper, cilantro, and scallions and mix well. Cook the bean mixture over medium heat until warm. Set aside.

2. Divide the lettuce among four large plates. Top the lettuce on each plate with the black bean mixture, tomatoes, corn, and avocado, followed by a spoonful or two of sour cream and as much of the remaining salsa as desired. Arrange some tortilla chips around the perimeter of the salads and place a bowl of tortilla chips on the table for those who want more.

Nutrition Analysis

Per serving: 460 calories, 21 g protein, 13 g total fat, 73 g carbohydrate, 14 g sugar, 21 g fiber

Greek Goddess Niçoise Salad

Makes 4 servings

Salad

16 ounces (455 g) small new potatoes, halved or cut into ½-inch (1 cm) pieces

Sea salt and fresh ground black pepper

8 ounces (225 g) green beans, trimmed and cut into 2-inch (5 cm) pieces

1 head romaine lettuce, shredded

1½ cups (246 g) cooked chickpeas or cannellini beans, or 1 (15-ounce [425 g]) can, rinsed and drained

1 cup (150 g) cherry or grape tomatoes, halved lengthwise

⅓ cup (33 g) pitted Kalamata olives, halved lengthwise

1 cup (235 ml) Tofu Feta (page 59), chopped

2 tablespoons (20 g) chopped red onion (optional)

Greek Goddess Dressing

¼ cup (60 ml) Tofu Feta (recipe follows)

2 tablespoons (30 g) tahini

2 tablespoons (30 ml) fresh lemon juice

2 tablespoons (30 ml) rice vinegar

2 tablespoons (30 ml) tamari

½ teaspoon onion powder

¼ teaspoon garlic powder

¼ cup (15 g) chopped fresh parsley

3 scallions, white and green parts, chopped

½ teaspoon dried oregano

1 tablespoon (7 g) ground golden flaxseeds

½ teaspoon sea salt

¼ teaspoon freshly ground black pepper

⅓ cup (70 ml) plain unsweetened plant milk

This recipe combines three of my salad favorites: Greek and Niçoise salad ingredients tossed with a creamy green goddess dressing. You can detect a slight Greek accent in the dressing thanks to the addition of tofu feta, lemon juice, and oregano.

(Continued)

(Continued)

1. Preheat the oven to 425°F (220°C). Line a rimmed baking sheet with parchment paper or a lightly coat with cooking spray.

2. To make the salad, arrange the potatoes on the baking sheet and spray with a little cooking spray. Season to taste with salt and pepper and roast until just softened and lightly browned, turning once, about 30 minutes. Remove the roasted potatoes from the oven and set aside to cool to room temperature.

3. While the potatoes are roasting, steam the green beans over boiling water until just tender, about 7 minutes. Run cold water over the cooked green beans to stop the cooking process, transfer to a bowl, and set aside.

4. In a large bowl, combine the lettuce, chickpeas, tomatoes, olives, and feta. Add the reserved potatoes and green beans. Sprinkle with the onion, if using.

5. To make the dressing, in a high-speed blender, combine the feta, tahini, lemon juice, vinegar, tamari, onion powder, garlic powder, parsley, scallions, oregano, flaxseeds, salt, and pepper. Blend until smooth and creamy. Blend in as much of the plant milk as needed to achieve a desired consistency. Taste and adjust the seasonings, if needed.

6. To serve, pour on as much of the dressing as desired and toss to combine. Serve immediately.

Nutrition Analysis

Per serving: 390 calories, 17 g protein, 15 g total fat, 50 g carbohydrate, 10 g sugar, 13 g fiber

Tofu Feta

3 tablespoons (45 ml) extra-virgin olive oil or water

3 tablespoons (45 ml) rice vinegar

3 tablespoons (45 ml) fresh lemon juice

1 teaspoon white miso paste

1 teaspoon sea salt

½ teaspoon dried oregano

12 to 16 ounces (340 to 455 g) extra-firm tofu, drained, well-pressed, and blotted dry

Marinated extra-firm tofu makes a delicious plant-based version of feta cheese.

1. In a bowl, combine the olive oil, vinegar, lemon juice, miso, salt, and oregano. Stir to mix well.

2. Cut the tofu into ½-inch (1 cm) dice and add it to the marinade, turning gently to coat well. Cover and set aside at room temperature for 1 hour. If not using right away, refrigerate until it is needed. It will keep well in the refrigerator for up to 5 days.

Nutrition Analysis

Per ¼-cup (37 g) serving (for 12 ounces [340 g] tofu): 90 calories, 4 g protein, 7 g total fat, 2 g carbohydrate, 0 g sugar, 0 g fiber

Per ¼-cup (37 g) serving (for 16 ounces [455 g] tofu): 100 calories, 6 g protein, 8 g total fat, 2 g carbohydrate, 0 g sugar, 0 g fiber

Tuscan Summer Pasta Salad

Makes 4 to 8 servings

Salad

8 ounces (225 g) gemelli or other bite-sized pasta

1½ cups (246 g) cooked chickpeas or cannellini beans, or 1 (15-ounce [425 g]) can, rinsed and drained

1 (6-ounce [168 g]) jar marinated artichoke hearts, drained

1 (6-ounce [168 g]) jar roasted red bell peppers, drained and chopped

1 carrot, shredded

1 cup (150 g) cherry or grape tomatoes, halved lengthwise

1 cup (20 g) baby arugula leaves

2 scallions, white and green parts, finely chopped

⅓ cup (33 g) pitted Kalamata olives, halved lengthwise

2 teaspoons capers, drained

¼ cup (10 g) chopped fresh basil leaves or chopped fresh parsley

Dressing

3 tablespoons (45 ml) balsamic vinegar

2 tablespoons (30 ml) fresh lemon juice

2 garlic cloves, crushed or coarsely chopped

1 tablespoon (16 g) almond butter

1 tablespoon (21 g) agave nectar or pure maple syrup

2 teaspoons hulled hemp seeds

1 teaspoon onion powder

1 teaspoon dried basil

½ teaspoon dried oregano

½ teaspoon sea salt

¼ teaspoon freshly ground black pepper

¼ cup (60 ml) water, as needed

You can make this salad ahead of time—just hold off on adding the dressing and fresh basil until you are ready to serve. The serving size will vary depending on whether you're enjoying this as a side dish or a main dish salad.

1. To make the salad, cook the pasta in a pot of boiling salted water until it is al dente. Drain and run under cold water, then drain again, and transfer to a large bowl. Add the chickpeas, artichokes, red peppers, carrot, tomatoes, arugula, scallions, olives, capers, and basil.

2. To make the dressing, in a blender, combine the balsamic vinegar, lemon juice, garlic, almond butter, agave, hemp seeds, onion powder, basil, oregano, salt, and pepper. Blend until smooth. Add as much of the water as needed to achieve a desired consistency. Blend again, then taste and adjust the seasonings, if needed.

3. To serve, pour as much of the dressing over the pasta salad as desired and toss to combine. Taste and adjust the seasonings, if needed.

Nutrition Analysis

Per serving [for 4]: 460 calories, 16 g protein, 11 g total fat, 76 g carbohydrate, 13 g sugar, 10 g fiber

Per serving [for 8]: 230 calories, 8 g protein, 6 g total fat, 38 g carbohydrate, 7 g sugar, 5 g fiber

Noodle Salad with Edamame and Sesame Dressing

Makes 4 to 6 servings

8 ounces (225 g) soba noodles

1½ cups (233 g) fresh or frozen shelled edamame

¼ cup (60 g) tahini

¼ cup (60 ml) plain unsweetened plant milk

2 tablespoons (30 ml) rice vinegar

1 tablespoon (15 ml) tamari

1 tablespoon (15 ml) fresh lime juice

1 tablespoon (7 g) ground golden flaxseeds

1 teaspoon sriracha sauce

1 teaspoon grated fresh ginger

1 teaspoon natural sugar

Sea salt and freshly ground black pepper

1 (12-ounce [350 g]) bag shredded cabbage

1 large carrot, shredded

½ cup (30 g) fresh cilantro leaves

2 scallions, white and green parts, minced

¼ cup (36 g) crushed unsalted dry-roasted peanuts

This hearty main-dish salad is loaded with flavor and is quick and easy to make. Bagged shredded cabbage makes short work of the prep. If you want your salad spicier, add more sriracha to the dressing.

1. Cook the soba in a pot of boiling salted water according to package directions. Drain and rinse with cold water. Transfer to a large bowl and set aside.

2. Cook the edamame in a small pot of boiling salted water until tender, about 10 minutes. Drain, rinsed under cold water, and set aside.

3. To make the dressing, in a blender, combine the tahini, plant milk, vinegar, tamari, lime juice, flaxseeds, sriracha, ginger, and sugar. Blend until smooth. Season with salt and pepper, then taste and adjust the seasonings if needed. Set aside.

4. To the bowl containing the soba, add the shredded cabbage, carrot, cilantro, scallions, and edamame. Pour on the dressing and toss well to combine. Sprinkle with the peanuts and serve immediately.

Nutrition Analysis

Per serving [for 4]: 480 calories, 24 g protein, 16 g total fat, 67 g carbohydrate, 6 g sugar, 8 g fiber

Per serving [for 6]: 320 calories, 16 g protein, 10 g total fat, 45 g carbohydrate, 4 g sugar, 5 g fiber

Plant-Power Buddha Bowls

Makes 4 servings

Dressing

1 roasted red pepper

1 tablespoon (16 g) almond butter

1 tablespoon (15 ml) fresh lemon juice

2 tablespoons (30 ml) water, plus more if needed

1 tablespoon (15 ml) tamari

2 tablespoons (8 g) nutritional yeast

2 teaspoons white miso paste

1 garlic clove, crushed or coarsely chopped

1 teaspoon agave nectar

½ teaspoon onion powder

½ teaspoon sea salt

¼ teaspoon freshly ground black pepper

Salad Bowls

4 cups packed (268 g) stemmed and finely chopped kale

2 cups (370 g) cooked quinoa or brown rice, warmed, if desired

1½ cups (200 g) Roasted Sweet Potatoes (page 66), warmed, if desired

1½ cups (258 g) cooked black beans, or 1 (15-ounce [425 g]) can, rinsed and drained, warmed, if desired

1 ripe Hass avocado, peeled, pitted, and diced

2 tablespoons (14 g) hulled hemp seeds

2 tablespoons (16 g) sunflower seed kernels

Sometimes called "hippie bowls," this main dish salad tastes great no matter what you call it. Make your dressing and components ahead of time and you can assemble it in minutes. If your beans, rice, and sweet potato are not already warm when serving, you may want to heat them. If you have some vegan bacon or roasted mushrooms on hand, either would make a good addition.

1. To prepare the dressing, in a blender or food processor, combine the red pepper, almond butter, lemon juice, water, tamari, nutritional yeast, miso, garlic, agave, onion powder, salt, and pepper. Blend until smooth and creamy. If the dressing is too thick, add more water, 1 tablespoon (15 ml) at a time, until a desired consistency is achieved. Set aside.

2. To make the salad bowls, divide the kale among four large shallow bowls. Top the kale with the cooked quinoa, sweet potato, black beans, and avocado. Drizzle with the dressing, sprinkle on the hemp seeds and sunflower seeds, and serve.

Nutrition Analysis

Per serving: 430 calories, 19 g protein, 16 g total fat, 59 g carbohydrate, 6 g sugar, 14 g fiber

Roasted Sweet Potatoes

Makes 4 servings

1 pound (454 g) sweet potatoes

1 tablespoon (15 ml) olive oil

Sea salt, to taste

Freshly ground black pepper, to taste

Roasting diced sweet potatoes brings out their delicious flavor. Enjoy them as a side or add to salads such as the Buddha bowls on page 65 or the rainbow salad on page 70.

1. Preheat the oven to 400°F (200°C).

2. Line a large rimmed baking sheet with parchment paper or coat with cooking spray.

3. Peel the sweet potatoes and cut them into ½-inch (1 cm) dice.

4. Spread the diced potato pieces in a single layer on the baking sheet. Drizzle with olive oil and season with sea salt and freshly ground black pepper.

5. Roast until tender, 20 to 30 minutes, stirring occasionally.

Curried Rice and Quinoa Salad

Makes 4 to 6 servings

2 cups (390 g) cooked and cooled brown basmati rice

1½ cups (278 g) cooked and cooled quinoa

1½ cups (246 g) cooked chickpeas, or 1 (15-ounce [425 g]) can, rinsed and drained

2 celery ribs, cut into ¼-inch (6 mm) dice

3 scallions, white and green parts, minced

1 carrot, shredded

1 red bell pepper, seeded and cut into ½-inch (1 cm) dice

⅓ cup (18 g) finely chopped fresh cilantro

1 ripe mango, peeled, seeded, and chopped

¼ cup (34 g) unsalted roasted cashew pieces

3 cups (108 g) green leaf lettuce, torn into bite size pieces

Dressing

2 tablespoons (30 ml) rice vinegar

2 tablespoons (32 g) almond butter

1 tablespoon (15 ml) fresh lime juice

1 tablespoon (21 g) agave nectar or pure maple syrup

1 tablespoon (6. 3 g) curry powder

½ teaspoon ground ginger

½ teaspoon garlic powder

½ teaspoon sea salt

⅛ teaspoon freshly ground black pepper

¼ cup (60 ml) water

Make this fragrant and colorful salad ahead of time to allow the flavors to blend. Spoon over lettuce when you are ready to serve.

1. In a large bowl, combine the rice, quinoa, chickpeas, celery, scallions, carrot, bell pepper, cilantro, mango, and cashews. Toss until well mixed. Set aside.

2. To make the dressing, in a blender, combine the vinegar, almond butter, lime juice, agave, curry powder, garlic powder, ginger, salt, and pepper. Blend until smooth. Add as much of the water as needed to achieve a desired consistency and blend again. Taste and adjust the seasonings, if needed.

3. To serve, pour the dressing over the salad and toss to combine. Divide the lettuce among shallow serving bowls and spoon the salad on top.

Nutrition Analysis

Per serving [for 4]: 480 calories, 16 g protein, 13 g total fat, 82 g carbohydrate, 22 g sugar, 13 g fiber

Per serving [for 6]: 320 calories, 11 g protein, 9 g total fat, 54 g carbohydrate, 15 g sugar, 9 g fiber

Chickpea Tuna Salad

½ cup (73g) sunflower seed kernels

1½ cups (246 g) cooked chickpeas, or 1 (15-ounce [425 g]) can, rinsed and drained

1 (6-ounce [168 g]) jar marinated artichoke hearts, well drained

½ cup (50 g) finely chopped celery

⅓ cup (48 g) finely chopped sweet or dill pickles

¼ cup (120 g) finely chopped red onion (optional)

¾ cup (175 ml) Cashew Mayo (page 182) or Soy Mayo (page 183)

2 teaspoons prepared yellow mustard

2 teaspoons fresh lemon juice

1 teaspoon dulse flakes (optional)

2 tablespoons (8 g) chopped fresh dill, or 2 teaspoons dried

½ teaspoon sea salt

¼ teaspoon freshly ground black pepper

Serve on a bed of lettuce or use as a filling for wraps or sandwiches. The dulse flakes are a sea vegetable that add a taste of the sea (and lots of nutrients) to this salad—look for it in natural food stores or online.

1. Cover the sunflower seeds in hot water and let soak for 3 hours. Drain and blot dry.

2. Blot dry the chickpeas and artichoke hearts and add them to a food processor with the sunflower seeds. Pulse a few times to chop the ingredients. Do not overprocess.

3. Transfer the chickpea mixture to a large bowl. Add the celery, pickles, and onion, if using.

4. In a small bowl, combine the mayo, mustard, lemon juice, dulse, if using, dill, salt, and pepper. Mix well, then scrape the dressing onto the salad and mix well. Taste and adjust the seasonings, if needed. Serve immediately, or cover and chill for several hours or overnight.

Nutrition Analysis

Per serving: 350 calories, 10 g protein, 24 g total fat, 27 g carbohydrate, 6 g sugar, 8 g fiber

PROTEIN PLUS

Rainbow Salad with Lemon Chia Dressing

Makes 4 servings

Salad

4 cups packed (120 g) baby spinach

1½ cups (338 g) diced roasted sweet potato

2 cups (390 g) cooked brown rice or quinoa, warmed

1½ cups (246 g) cooked chickpeas, or 1 (15-ounce [425 g]) can, rinsed and drained

½ cup (55 g) toasted slivered almonds or walnut pieces

1 cup (150 g) shredded red cabbage

1 large Gala or Fuji apple, cored and diced

1 ripe Hass avocado, peeled, pitted, and diced

Dressing

2 tablespoons (32 g) almond butter

2 tablespoons (30 ml) fresh lemon juice

1 tablespoon (15 ml) rice vinegar

⅓ cup (70 ml) water, plus more if needed

2 teaspoons pure maple syrup

2 teaspoons ground chia seeds

Sea salt and freshly ground black pepper

This colorful main-dish salad is a great way to use leftover grains: warm up whatever you have on hand. If you also roast the sweet potatoes ahead of time, this salad can come together quickly. For even more protein, add some diced smoked tofu.

1. To make the salad, in a large bowl, combine the spinach, roasted sweet potatoes, brown rice, chickpeas, almonds, cabbage, apple, and avocado.

2. To make the dressing, in a blender, combine the almond butter, lemon juice, vinegar, water, maple syrup, and chia seeds. Blend until smooth. Season to taste with salt and black pepper. Set aside for 5 minutes before using. Taste and adjust the seasonings, if needed. If the dressing is too thick, add more water, 1 tablespoon at a time.

3. To serve, drizzle the dressing on the salad and toss well to coat.

Nutrition Analysis

Per serving: 530 calories, 16 g protein, 21 g total fat, 74 g carbohydrate, 12 g sugar, 15 g fiber

Chapter 4
Super Sandwiches

Tempeh Avocado Reubens

Makes 2 sandwiches

4 slices sprouted whole-grain bread, toasted

2 tablespoons (30 ml) Soy Mayonnaise (page 183) or other vegan mayo

1 ripe Hass avocado, peeled, pitted, and thinly sliced

8 ounces (225 g) Braised Tempeh (page 167), cut into ¼-inch (6 mm) strips

1 cup (235 ml) firmly packed sauerkraut, well drained and warmed

Braised tempeh is terrific in a Reuben sandwich because it is a good complement to the sauerkraut. Although rye bread is traditional, sprouted whole-grain bread will provide more protein and other nutrients. Sliced avocado replaces the cheese in this recipe, but you can use sliced vegan cheese, if you prefer.

1. Spread ½ tablespoon (7 ml) of mayo on 2 slices of toasted bread and place on a cutting board, mayo side up. Top each bread slice equally with avocado, tempeh, and warm sauerkraut.

2. Spread mayo on one side of the remaining two toasted bread slices. Place the bread slices on top of the sandwiches, mayo-side down.

3. Cut each sandwich in half and serve immediately.

Nutrition Analysis

Per serving: 370 calories, 19 g protein, 16 g total fat, 42 g carbohydrate, 2 g sugar, 13 g fiber

Sloppy Lentils and 'Shrooms

Makes 4 servings

2 tablespoons (30 ml) water, or 1 tablespoon (15 ml) extra-virgin olive oil

½ cup (80 g) finely chopped yellow onion

1 cup (70 g) chopped mushrooms (any type)

2 cups (384 g) cooked green or brown lentils, well drained

1 (14-ounce [397 g]) can tomato sauce or puree

2 tablespoons (30 ml) pure maple syrup

2 tablespoons (30 ml) cider vinegar

2 tablespoons (30 ml) tamari

1 tablespoon (16 g) tomato paste

1 tablespoon (11 g) yellow mustard

½ teaspoon sea salt

¼ teaspoon freshly ground black pepper

¼ teaspoon ground cayenne

¼ teaspoon smoked paprika

1 teaspoon liquid smoke

4 whole-grain sprouted sandwich rolls, split and toasted

Cooked lentils combine with chopped mushrooms in a sweet and savory sauce for a super sloppy Joe sandwich. This versatile sandwich filling can be made with chopped seitan, steamed crumbled tempeh, or shredded jackfruit. You could also skip the 'shrooms and go with all lentils or another type of bean.

1. Heat the water in a large saucepan over medium heat. Add the onion and cook until softened, about 5 minutes. Add the mushrooms and cook, stirring, until softened and lightly browned, 5 minutes. Add the cooked lentils, then stir in the tomato sauce, maple syrup, vinegar, tamari, tomato paste, mustard, salt, pepper, cayenne, and paprika. Stir to mix well.

2. Simmer for 15 to 20 minutes, stirring occasionally, until the sauce reduces to a desired consistency. Near the end of the cooking time, stir in the liquid smoke, then taste and adjust the seasonings, if needed to balance the flavors.

3. To serve, spoon the lentil mixture onto the toasted rolls. Serve hot.

Nutrition Analysis

Per serving: 350 calories, 21 g protein, 2.5 g total fat, 70 g carbohydrate, 14 g sugar, 16 g fiber

Seitan and Mushroom Gyros

Makes 2 gyros

Sauce

¼ cup (60 ml) Cashew Mayo (page 182) or other vegan mayo

1 tablespoon (7 g) hulled hemp seeds

1 tablespoon (15 ml) fresh lemon juice

½ teaspoon garlic powder

½ teaspoon dried oregano

½ teaspoon dried dill weed

¼ teaspoon freshly ground black pepper

Gyros

3 garlic cloves, crushed or coarsely chopped

2 tablespoons (30 ml) fresh lemon juice

1½ tablespoons (23 ml) tamari

1 tablespoon (15 ml) water

1 tablespoon (20 g) maple syrup

2 teaspoons dried oregano

1 teaspoon garlic powder

¼ teaspoon freshly ground black pepper

8 ounces (225 g) Baked Seitan (page 168), thinly sliced

1 large portobello mushroom cap, cut into ¼-inch (6 mm) thick strips

2 tablespoons (30 ml) water, or 1 tablespoon (15 ml) extra-virgin olive oil

4 whole-grain or sprouted-grain pita breads or tortillas

Tomato slices, cucumber slices, baby spinach leaves or shredded lettuce, red onion slivers

If you're not a fan of seitan, substitute tofu or tempeh, or use all portobello mushrooms. Food for Life Ezekiel Bread makes sprouted grain pocket breads (pitas) and tortillas.

1. To make the sauce, combine all the sauce ingredients in a small bowl. Mix well, then taste and adjust the seasonings, if needed. Set aside. If not using right away, cover and refrigerate until you are ready to use it.

2. To make the gyros, in a large shallow bowl, combine the garlic, lemon juice, tamari, water, maple syrup, oregano, garlic powder, and black pepper and mix well. Add the sliced seitan and mushroom and toss with the marinade. Set aside to marinate for at least 30 minutes or overnight.

3. Heat the water in a large skillet over medium heat. Transfer the seitan and mushrooms to the hot skillet, in batches, if needed, to prevent overcrowding. Sauté for about 5 minutes or until nicely browned, adding any remaining marinade to the pan.

4. To serve, arrange tomato slices, cucumber slices, spinach leaves, and onion slivers in the center of each pita. Spoon the reserved sauce on top of the vegetables. Arrange the seitan and mushrooms strips on top. Fold the sides of each pita to overlap and serve immediately.

Nutrition Analysis

Per serving: 380 calories, 34 g protein, 8 g total fat, 50 g carbohydrate, 8 g sugar, 6 g fiber

Note:

To keep the sandwich closed you can wrap the bottom half of each filled pita with sandwich paper or secure it with kitchen twine or large sandwich picks.

Variation:
Top the burgers with a slice of vegan cheese and tempeh bacon for added flavor and protein.

Bean and Beet Burgers

Makes 6 servings

1½ cups (258 g) cooked black beans, or 1 (15-ounce [425 g]) can, rinsed, drained, and blotted dry

½ cup (60 g) chopped walnuts

½ cup (78 g) old-fashioned rolled oats, plus more if needed

½ cup (93 g) cooked quinoa or brown rice, drained, if needed, and blotted dry

⅓ cup (70 ml) chopped pickled beets, drained and blotted dry

¼ cup (40 g) minced yellow onion

2 tablespoons (18 g) vital wheat gluten, plus more if needed

2 tablespoons (14 g) ground golden flaxseed

2 teaspoons tomato paste

½ teaspoon garlic powder

½ teaspoon onion powder

½ teaspoon smoked paprika

½ teaspoon sea salt

¼ teaspoon freshly ground black pepper

Dried bread crumbs (optional)

6 sprouted whole-grain burger rolls

Burger condiments, such as ketchup, mustard, vegan mayonnaise, to serve

Plant-based burgers are popping up all over—even in mainstream fast-food restaurants. It's great to have choices when you're on the road, but I prefer the home-made goodness of a burger like this one that's high in protein and low in fat. Featuring black beans, walnuts, oats, and pickled beets, these burgers have a great flavor and firm texture that holds up well when cooked. The wheat gluten will make firmer burgers, but it's okay to leave it out if you're gluten intolerant.

1. In a food processor, combine the beans, walnuts, oats, quinoa, beets, and onion, and process until well combined. Add the wheat gluten, flaxseeds, tomato paste, garlic powder, onion powder, paprika, salt, and pepper. Process to mix well. Transfer the mixture to a work surface and divide the mixture into six balls (more or less, depending on how large you like your burgers). If the mixture is too soft to hold its shape, add a little more vital wheat gluten, oats, or bread crumbs. Use your hands to firmly shape each ball into a thin burger, pressing the mixture well to hold the burger together. Set the burgers aside on a plate and refrigerate for 1 hour or overnight. (The burgers can also be frozen at this point for later use.)

2. Preheat the oven to 400°F (200°C). Line a rimmed baking sheet with parchment paper or coat with cooking spray.

3. Arrange the burgers on the baking sheet. Spray the burgers with cooking spray and bake for 20 minutes. Use a spatula to flip the burgers and bake for 15 to 20 minutes longer.

4. Remove from the oven and let cool for about 5 minutes before serving on burger rolls with your favorite condiments.

Nutrition Analysis

Per serving: 370 calories, 19 g protein, 10 g total fat, 58 g carbohydrate, 3 g sugar, 13 g fiber

Plant-Powered Club Sandwiches

Makes 2 sandwiches

2 tablespoons (30 ml) Cashew Mayo (page 182) or store-bought vegan mayo

1 teaspoon Dijon mustard

4 slices sprouted whole-grain bread, toasted

8 lettuce or spinach leaves

8 thin slices Ham I Am (page 174) or other vegan ham

6 thin slices tomato

½ teaspoon Everything Seasoning (page 38) or sea salt and freshly ground black pepper

1 ripe Hass avocado, peeled, pitted, and thinly sliced

8 strips cooked Tempeh Bacon (page 173)

These club sandwiches feature plant-based ham, bacon, and mayo, all in one delicious sandwich. The recipe is easily doubled to make more sandwiches. The amount of ham to use depends on how thinly you slice it and personal preference.

1. In a small bowl, combine the mayo with the mustard until blended. Spread about ½ tablespoon (7 g) on one side of each slice of toasted bread.

2. Place two of the bread slices on a work surface, mayo-side up, top each with two lettuce leaves, followed by 4 ham slices, 3 tomato slices, ¼ teaspoon Everything Seasoning, avocado slices, and 4 bacon slices. Top each sandwich with the remaining lettuce leaves and the remaining toast (mayo-side down). Secure each sandwich with a long sandwich pick and cut each sandwich in half.

Nutrition Analysis

Per serving: 630 calories, 34 g protein, 29 g total fat, 63 g carbohydrate, 16 g sugar, 13 g fiber

Seitan Cheesesteaks

Makes 2 sandwiches

2 tablespoons (30 ml) water, or 1 tablespoon (15 ml) neutral-tasting oil, such as avocado oil

6 ounces (168 g) Baked Seitan (page 168), thinly sliced

1 yellow onion, thinly sliced

1 red bell pepper, seeded and thinly sliced

1 large portobello mushroom cap, thinly sliced

⅓ cup (80 g) ketchup

1 tablespoon (15 ml) vegan Worcestershire sauce or tamari

Sea salt and freshly ground black pepper

¾ cup (175 ml) Easy Cheesy Sauce (page 44), warmed

2 (6-inch [15 cm]) sub rolls, split and toasted

A plant-based version of the classic Philadelphia cheesesteak sandwich is easier than you might think. All it takes is thinly sliced portobello mushrooms and seitan, onions, and bell peppers topped with some creamy, cheesy sauce, all loaded into a crusty sub roll.

1. Heat the water in a large skillet over medium-high heat. Add the seitan and cook, turning occasionally, until browned, about 5 minutes. Remove the seitan from the skillet and set aside.

2. Reheat the same skillet over medium-high heat. Add the onion and cook until softened, about 5 minutes. Add the bell pepper, mushroom, and a splash of water and cook, stirring occasionally, to soften, about 5 minutes. Stir in the ketchup and Worcestershire sauce, and season with salt and pepper to taste.

3. Cook for 5 minutes longer to combine the flavors. Return the seitan to the skillet and cook for 5 minutes to heat through. Spoon about half of the warm cheesy sauce onto the seitan mixture and keep warm while you toast the rolls.

4. To serve, divide the seitan mixture between the two rolls and top each with some of the remaining cheesy sauce. Serve hot.

Nutrition Analysis

Per serving: 670 calories, 54 g protein, 12 g total fat, 89 g carbohydrate, 20 g sugar, 9 g fiber

Tofu Banh Mi

Makes 2 sandwiches

½ cup (55 g) shredded carrot

1½ tablespoons (23 ml) rice vinegar

¾ teaspoon natural sugar

⅛ teaspoon sea salt

1 tablespoon (15 ml) neutral-tasting vegetable oil, such as avocado oil

8 ounces (225 g) extra-firm tofu, drained, blotted dry and thinly sliced

⅓ cup (70 ml) hoisin sauce

2 (6-inch [15 cm]) whole-grain sub rolls, split and lightly toasted

¼ cup (60 ml) Cashew Mayo (page 182) or store-bought vegan mayo

1 tablespoon (15 ml) sriracha, plus more as needed

8 thin cucumber slices

1½ tablespoons (23 ml) chopped bottled jalapeño slices

½ cup (30 g) fresh cilantro leaves

The banh mi is hands-down my favorite sandwich. It's hard to resist a toasted roll filled with crisp veggies, hoisin-glazed tofu, fragrant cilantro, spicy sriracha, and creamy mayo.

1. In a small bowl, combine the shredded carrot, vinegar, sugar, and salt. Mix well and set aside.

2. Heat the oil in a skillet over medium heat. Add the tofu slices and cook until lightly browned, turning frequently, about 5 minutes. Spoon the hoisin onto the tofu slices, turning to coat and glaze the slices for another minute or two. Remove from the heat and set aside to cool.

3. To assemble the sandwiches, spread the inside of each sub roll with mayo and drizzle with sriracha. Arrange one-half of the tofu slices on the bottom half of each baguette. Top each with 4 cucumber slices, half the jalapeños, half the cilantro, and the half the pickled carrot. Close up the sandwiches and serve at once.

Nutrition Analysis

Per serving: 650 calories, 23 g protein, 28 g total fat, 78 g carbohydrate, 19 g sugar, 2 g fiber

Sweet Potato and Tempeh Burritos

Makes 4 servings

2 tablespoons (30 ml) water, or 1 tablespoon (15 ml) neutral-tasting vegetable oil, such as avocado oil

1 sweet potato, peeled and cut into thin strips

8 ounces (225 g) Braised Tempeh (page 167), cut into ¼-inch (6 mm) strips

1 red bell pepper, seeded and cut into thin strips

½ teaspoon chili powder

½ teaspoon onion powder

½ teaspoon garlic powder

Sea salt and freshly ground black pepper

3 cups (90 g) fresh baby spinach leaves

4 sprouted whole-grain tortillas

Tomato-based salsa

I love the way the bright flavor of the sweet potato plays against the spicy salsa and seasoned tempeh. Spinach and whole-grain tortillas make these burritos a hearty and healthy meal.

1. Heat the water in a large skillet over medium heat. Add the sweet potato and cook for 5 minutes to soften. Add the tempeh and red bell pepper. Sprinkle with the chili powder, onion powder, garlic powder, and salt and pepper to taste.

2. Cook, stirring occasionally, until the vegetables are tender, about 10 minutes longer, adding a little more water, if needed, so the vegetables and tempeh don't burn. Stir in the baby spinach and cook until the spinach is wilted and any remaining liquid is evaporated, 1 to 2 minutes. Remove from the heat.

3. Arrange the tortillas on a flat surface. Spoon the filling down the center of each tortilla, dividing evenly. Top the filling with a spoonful of your favorite salsa. Roll up the tortilla around the filling.

4. Heat a dry nonstick skillet over medium heat. One at a time, place each burrito seam-side down in the skillet to seal the seam, and then flipped it for a minute to get both sides a little crisped. Repeat with remaining burritos. To serve, cut the burritos in half and serve immediately with more salsa on the side for dipping.

Nutrition Analysis

Per serving: 250 calories, 12 g protein, 6 g total fat, 38 g carbohydrate, 5 g sugar, 8 g fiber

Black and White Bean Quesadillas

Makes 4 servings

1½ cups (265 g) cooked great Northern or other white beans, or 1 (15-ounce [425g]) can, rinsed and drained

1 cup (235 ml) tomato-based salsa, plus more to serve

⅓ cup (21 g) nutritional yeast

½ teaspoon onion powder

½ teaspoon garlic powder

½ teaspoon ground coriander

½ teaspoon ground cumin

¼ teaspoon chili powder

Sea salt and freshly ground black pepper

1 cup (256 g) cooked or canned black beans, drained and rinsed

4 large whole-grain flour tortillas

No cheese needed in quesadillas made with two kinds of beans seasoned with salsa, nutritional yeast, and zesty spices.

1. In a food processor, combine the white beans, ½ cup (120 ml) of the salsa, the nutritional yeast, onion powder, garlic powder, coriander, cumin, chili powder, and salt and pepper to taste. Pulse until well combined. Transfer the white bean mixture into a bowl. Add the black beans and the remaining ½ cup (120 ml) of salsa and stir to combine.

2. Arrange the four tortillas on a flat work surface. Divide the filling mixture evenly among the tortillas. Spread the filling mixture evenly on half of each tortilla. Fold the remaining half of each tortilla over the filling and press gently to enclose and spread the filling close to the edges.

3. Heat a large nonstick skillet over medium heat. Arrange two of the quesadillas in the hot dry skillet, (or just one at a time, depending on the size of your skillet). Flatten the quesadillas with a spatula and cook until browned on the bottom, 2 to 3 minutes. Flip the quesadillas and cook until the other side is golden brown, 2 to 3 minutes. Repeat with remaining quesadillas. Cut into wedges to serve with additional salsa on the side.

Nutrition Analysis

Per serving: 480 calories, 25 g protein, 9 g total fat, 77 g carbohydrate, 7 g sugar, 20 g fiber

PROTEIN PLUS

Tofu Tacos with Sriracha-Lime Slaw

Makes 4 to 6 tacos

3 cups (210 g) shredded green cabbage

2 tablespoons (8 g) chopped fresh cilantro leaves

⅓ cup (90 ml) Cashew Mayo (page 182) or store-bought vegan mayo

2 tablespoons (30 ml) fresh lime juice

2 teaspoons sriracha

1½ teaspoons natural sugar

¼ teaspoon ground cumin

¼ teaspoon ground coriander

Sea salt

Baked Marinated Tofu (page 176), cut into strips

½ teaspoon chili powder

½ teaspoon smoked paprika

4 to 6 sprouted whole-grain tortillas (or your preferred tortillas)

1 ripe Hass avocado, peeled, pitted, and cut into strips

A zesty slaw adds texture and flavor to these tacos filled with marinated baked tofu and creamy avocado.

1. In a bowl, combine the cabbage and cilantro. In a small bowl, combine the mayo, lime juice, sriracha, sugar, ½ teaspoon salt, cumin, and coriander. Add the dressing to the cabbage and mix well to combine. Set aside. If you are not using the slaw right away, cover and refrigerate it until it is needed.

2. Put the baked tofu into a mixing bowl. Add the chili powder and paprika, and season with salt to taste. Toss to combine.

3. To serve, warm the tortillas, then arrange a few tofu strips and avocado strips inside each tortilla. Add about ½ cup (120 ml) of the slaw on each and serve.

Nutrition Analysis

Per serving [for 4 tortillas]: 420 calories, 19 g protein, 18 g total fat, 49 g carbohydrate, 15 g sugar, 10 g fiber

Per serving [for 6 tortillas]: 330 calories, 15 g protein, 13 g total fat, 41 g carbohydrate, 10 g sugar, 8 g fiber

Chapter 5
Stovetop Simmers and Skillets

Moroccan Lentil and Chickpea Soup

Makes 4 servings

¼ (60 ml) cup water

1 yellow onion, finely chopped

2 carrots, finely chopped

1 celery rib, finely chopped

3 garlic cloves, minced

1 tablespoon (8 g) grated fresh ginger

1 tablespoon (15 ml) Harissa Spice Blend (see opposite)

1 teaspoon ground turmeric

¼ teaspoon ground cinnamon

1 teaspoon sea salt

¼ teaspoon freshly ground black pepper

½ cup (93 g) long-grain brown rice

1 (28-ounce [794 g]) can diced tomatoes with its juice

6 to 8 cups (1.5 to 2 L) vegetable broth

1¼ cups (240 g) brown lentils, rinsed

3 cups (492 g) cooked chickpeas, or 2 (15-ounce [425 g]) cans, rinsed and drained

1 tablespoon (15 ml) fresh lemon juice

1 cup (60 g) chopped fresh parsley or cilantro

This protein-packed soup combines lentils, chickpeas, and brown rice in a spicy broth laced with fiery harissa. It has the added bonus of making your house smell wonderful as it simmers. For a milder soup, use less harissa or omit it entirely.

1. Heat the water in a large soup pot over medium heat. Add the onion, carrots, and celery and cook for 5 minutes to soften, stirring occasionally.

2. Reduce the heat to low and stir in the garlic, ginger, harissa, turmeric, cinnamon, salt, and pepper. Cook, stirring constantly, until fragrant, 1 minute.

3. Add the rice and tomatoes, then stir in 6 cups (1.5 L) of the broth and bring to a boil; reduce the heat to a simmer. Add the lentils and chickpeas, cover, and simmer until the lentils and rice are tender, about 45 minutes. Stir in as much of the remaining 2 cups (475 ml) broth as needed to achieve a desired consistency (it should be fairly thick).

4. Stir in the lemon juice and cook for 5 minutes. Stir in the fresh parsley and serve hot.

Nutrition Analysis

Per serving: 400 calories, 22 g protein, 3.5 g total fat, 74 g carbohydrate, 13 g sugar, 20 g fiber

Harissa
Spice Blend

Makes about ½ cup (120 ml)

2 tablespoons (10 g) coriander seeds

2 tablespoons (13 g) caraway seed

1 tablespoon (6 g) cumin seed

1 tablespoon (3.6 g) red pepper flakes

2 teaspoons smoked paprika

2 teaspoons garlic powder

1 teaspoon sea salt

Use this spicy and fragrant North African spice blend in the Moroccan Lentil and Chickpea Soup (opposite).

1. Combine the coriander seeds, caraway seeds, cumin seeds, and red pepper flakes in a spice grinder and grind to a powder.

2. Transfer to a small bowl or a jar with a tight-fitting lid and add the paprika, garlic powder, and salt, stirring to mix well.

3. Cover tightly and store at room temperature for up to 6 months.

Nutrition Analysis

Per 1-tablespoon (6 g) serving: 20 calories, 1 g protein, 1 g total fat, 3 g carbohydrate, 0 g sugar, 2 g fiber

Black Bean Soup with Tempeh Bacon

Makes 4 servings

2 tablespoons (30 ml) water, or 1 tablespoon (15 ml) extra-virgin olive oil

1 yellow onion, finely chopped

3 garlic cloves, minced

1 (14.5-ounce [411 g]) can diced fire-roasted tomatoes with its juice

3 tablespoons (32 g) red quinoa, rinsed

1 teaspoon smoked paprika

½ teaspoon dried oregano

½ teaspoon chipotle chile powder, plus more if needed

Sea salt and freshly ground black pepper

4 cups (946 ml) vegetable broth

3 cups (516 g) cooked black beans, or 2 (15-ounce [425 g]) cans, rinsed and drained

½ teaspoon liquid smoke

½ cup (120 ml) chopped Tempeh Bacon (page 173)

Cashew Sour Cream (page 180), diced avocado, crumbled corn chips, to garnish (optional)

Nothing says "plant protein" quite like a hearty bowl of black bean soup topped with tempeh bacon. A small amount of quinoa adds body and texture, while a dash of chipotle chile powder and a splash of liquid smoke add depth of flavor.

1. Heat the water in a large saucepan over medium-high heat. Add the onion and cook for 5 minutes to soften. Add the garlic, tomatoes, quinoa, paprika, oregano, chipotle powder, and salt and pepper to taste. Cook, stirring, for 1 minute, then add the broth and beans, and bring to a boil. Reduce the heat to a simmer and cook for 30 minutes, or until the vegetables are soft and the flavors are well blended.

2. Just before serving, stir in the liquid smoke, then taste and adjust the seasonings, adding more salt and chipotle chile, if needed. Ladle into bowls and serve hot topped with tempeh bacon and garnishes, if desired.

Nutrition Analysis

Per serving: 310 calories, 17 g protein, 5 g total fat, 52 g carbohydrate, 10 g sugar, 14 g fiber

White Bean Soup with Kale and Sausage

Makes 4 servings

2 tablespoons (30 ml) water, or 1 tablespoon (15 ml) neutral-tasting oil, such as avocado oil

3 links Plant-Perfect Sausage (page 170) or store-bought vegan sausage, cut into ¼-inch (6 mm) slices

1 yellow onion, finely chopped

4 to 5 garlic cloves, minced

6 cups (1.5 ml) vegetable broth

16 ounces (455 g) Yukon gold potatoes, cut into 1-inch (2.5 cm) cubes

3 tablespoons (12 g) nutritional yeast

1 tablespoon (7 g) smoked paprika

1 teaspoon dried oregano

¼ to ½ teaspoon red pepper flakes

1 bay leaf

Sea salt and freshly ground black pepper

1½ cups (266 g) cooked cannellini beans or other white beans, or 1 (15-ounce [425 g]) can, rinsed and drained

8 ounces (225 g) kale, tough stems removed, finely chopped

Sea salt and freshly ground black pepper

2 tablespoons (30 ml) dry sherry (optional)

1 tablespoon (15 ml) fresh lemon juice (optional)

Inspired by the Portuguese soup, caldo verde, this flavorful potion features white beans, kale, lots of garlic, and a splash of sherry. The addition of plant-based sausage is a nod to the original version. If you're not a fan of heat, you can omit the red pepper flakes.

1. Heat the water in a large pot over medium heat. Add the sausage and cook until browned, about 3 minutes. Remove the sausage from the pot and set aside.

2. In the same pot, combine the onion, garlic, and ½ cup (60 ml) of the broth. Cook until the onion is softened, about 5 minutes. Add the potatoes, nutritional yeast, paprika, oregano, red pepper flakes, and bay leaf. Stir in the remaining 5½ cups (1.3 L) broth and add salt and pepper to taste. Bring to a boil over high heat, then reduce the heat to a simmer and cook for 15 minutes. Add the beans, kale, and reserved sausage and continue to simmer until the vegetables are tender, 5 to 10 minutes.

3. Remove and discard the bay leaf. Stir in the sherry and lemon juice, if using. Taste and adjust the seasonings, if needed. Serve hot.

Nutrition Analysis

Per serving: 360 calories, 27 g protein, 5 g total fat, 55 g carbohydrate, 7 g sugar, 13 g fiber

Tofu Ramen Bowls

Makes 4 servings

1 cup (63 g) snow peas or small broccoli florets

2 tablespoons (30 ml) water, or 1 tablespoon (15 ml) neutral-tasting vegetable oil, such as avocado oil

4 ounces (115 g) fresh shiitake mushroom caps, sliced

3 tablespoons (45 ml) tamari

1 small yellow onion, thinly sliced

1 carrot, thinly sliced

2 garlic cloves, minced

1 tablespoon (8 g) grated fresh ginger

8 to 12 cups (1.8 to 2.8 L) vegetable broth (depending on how brothy you like your soup)

1 tablespoon (16 g) white miso paste

1 tablespoon (15 ml) mirin

1 teaspoon dark sesame oil (optional)

8 ounces (225 g) ramen noodles

4 cups (280 g) thinly sliced bok choy or other greens (spinach is good)

Baked Marinated Tofu (page 176), cut into thin strips

2 scallions, white and green parts, thinly sliced

1 tablespoon (8 g) toasted white or black sesame seeds

Sriracha, garlic chili paste, or hot chili oil, to garnish (optional)

Ramen bowls are a quick and easy way to enjoy loads of veggies with chewy noodles in a savory broth. If you're not a fan of tofu, substitute edamame or sliced seitan. If using ramen noodle bricks, be sure to throw away their enclosed seasoning packets—they're usually loaded with MSG.

1. Blanch the snow peas in boiling water until bright green and slightly softened, 1 minute. Drain and transfer to a bowl of ice water to stop the cooking process. Drain and set aside.

2. Heat the water in a large pot over medium-high heat. Add the shiitakes and 1 tablespoon (15 ml) of the tamari and cook, stirring, until the mushrooms are tender and browned. Remove the mushrooms from the pot and set aside.

3. To the same pot, add the onion, carrot, garlic, and ginger and ½ cup (120 ml) of the vegetable broth. Cook for 5 minutes, stirring occasionally. Reserve 2 tablespoons (30 ml) of the remaining broth and stir in as much of the remaining vegetable broth as desired. Stir in the remaining 2 tablespoons (30 ml) tamari. Bring to a boil, then reduce the heat to low and simmer for 20 minutes.

4. In a small bowl, combine the miso paste, mirin, sesame oil (if using), and the reserved 2 tablespoons (30 ml) of the broth, stirring until blended. Scrape the mixture into the pot with the broth and keep at a low simmer while you proceed with the recipe.

(Continued)

(Continued)

5. In a small bowl, combine the miso paste, mirin, sesame oil (if using), and the reserved 2 tablespoons (30 ml) of the broth, stirring until blended. Scrape the mixture into the pot with the broth and keep at a low simmer while you proceed with the recipe.

6. Add the noodles to the broth. Cover and cook for about 3 minutes or according to package directions. Scoop the noodles out of the broth and divide among four large soup bowls. To the simmering broth, add the bok choy and cook for 2 minutes, or until wilted.

7. Scoop out the bok choy and arrange in one section on top of the noodles in each bowl. Arrange the reserved shiitakes next to the bok choy in each bowl, followed by a few slices of baked tofu next to the shiitakes. Arrange a few snow peas next to the shiitakes in each bowl, then ladle the hot broth into the bowls.

8. Sprinkle each bowl with scallions, sesame seeds, and a little sriracha, if desired, and serve.

Nutrition Analysis

Per serving: 490 calories, 23 g protein, 16 g total fat, 67 g carbohydrate, 20 g sugar, 3 g fiber

Three-Bean Chili

Makes 4 to 6 servings

1 yellow onion, minced

1 carrot, minced

1 red bell pepper, seeded and minced

3 garlic cloves, minced

2½ (590 ml) cups vegetable broth or water

1 (28-ounce [794 g]) can crushed tomatoes

2 tablespoons (15 g) chili powder

1 teaspoon smoked paprika

1 teaspoon ground cumin

1 teaspoon onion powder

½ teaspoon oregano

1 teaspoon sea salt

¼ teaspoon freshly ground black pepper

3 cups (531 g) cooked dark red kidney beans, or 2 (15-ounce [425 g]) cans, rinsed and drained

1½ cups (258 g) cooked black beans, or 1 (15-ounce [425 g]) can, rinsed and drained

1½ cups (257 g) cooked pinto beans, or 1 (15-ounce [425 g]) can, rinsed and drained

⅓ cup (70 ml) barbecue sauce

2 cups (328 g) fresh or frozen corn kernels

1 ripe Hass avocado, peeled, pitted, and diced, to garnish (optional)

Mix and match your favorite beans to make this hearty chili. The additions of barbecue sauce and corn kernels add a pop of sweetness and a nice depth of flavor.

1. In a large pot over medium heat, combine the onion, carrot, bell pepper, garlic, and ½ cup (120 ml) of the broth. Cook until the vegetables are softened, about 5 minutes. Add the tomatoes, chili powder, cumin, onion powder, oregano, salt, and pepper and the remaining 2 cups (475 ml) of the broth. Bring to a boil then reduce heat to a simmer. Stir in the kidney beans, black beans, pinto beans, and barbecue sauce. Cover to prevent spatters, if desired. Simmer until the vegetables are tender and the flavors have combined, stirring occasionally, about 30 minutes.

2. Stir in the corn kernels. Taste and adjust the seasonings, if needed. Cook for 5 to 10 minutes longer. Serve hot, garnished with avocado, if using.

Nutrition Analysis

Per serving: 380 calories, 21 g protein, 2.5 g total fat, 77 g carbohydrate, 16 g sugar, 20 g fiber

PROTEIN PLUS

Tortilla Soup with Pinto Beans and Tempeh

Makes 6 servings

3 cups (710 ml) vegetable broth or water, plus more as needed

3 garlic cloves, minced

1 teaspoon chili powder

1 (24-ounce [680 g]) jar chunky tomato-based salsa (mild or hot)

3 cups (513 g) cooked pinto beans, or 2 (15-ounce [425 g]) cans, rinsed and drained

8 ounces (225 g) Braised Tempeh (page 167), cut into ½-inch (1 cm) dice

1½ cups (246 g) frozen corn kernels

Sea salt and freshly ground pepper

2 scallions, white and green parts, minced

2 tablespoons (8 g) chopped fresh cilantro

1 tablespoon (15 ml) fresh lime juice

2 cups (475 ml) crushed tortilla chips, plus more to serve

Tempeh and pinto beans bring a wealth of protein to this thick and savory soup. If you don't want to use tempeh, you can leave it out and add more beans.

1. Heat ½ cup (120 ml) of the broth in a large saucepan over medium heat. Add the garlic and cook until fragrant, 30 seconds. Stir in the chili powder, then add the salsa, beans, tempeh, corn, and remaining 2½ cups (590 ml) of broth. Season to taste with salt and pepper. Bring to a boil, then reduce the heat to a simmer, and cook for 5 minutes.

2. Remove from the heat and stir in the scallions, cilantro, and lime juice. Taste and adjust the seasonings, if needed. If the soup is too thick, add more broth. Top with the tortilla chips and serve hot, with more tortilla chips at the table.

Nutrition Analysis

Per serving: 370 calories, 19 g protein, 9 g total fat, 58 g carbohydrate, 10 g sugar, 12 g fiber

Brunswick Stew

Makes 4 to 6 servings

2 tablespoons (30 ml) water, or 1 tablespoon (15 ml) extra-virgin olive oil

3 Plant-Perfect Sausages (page 170), cut into ½-inch [1 cm] pieces

1 yellow onion, finely chopped

3 cups (710 ml) vegetable broth

1 cup (192 g) green lentils, rinsed

2 large white potatoes, diced

2 garlic cloves, minced

2 teaspoons grated fresh ginger

1 (14.5-ounce [411 g]) can fire-roasted diced tomatoes with its juice

1 (16-ounce [455 g]) package frozen succotash

3 tablespoons (45 ml) vegan Worcestershire sauce or tamari

2 teaspoons prepared yellow mustard

1 teaspoon natural sugar

¼ teaspoon ground allspice

½ teaspoon Tabasco sauce

Sea salt and freshly ground black pepper

½ teaspoon liquid smoke

This homey Southern stew is generally made with whatever proteins are at hand—in this case, it happens to be lentils and plant-based sausage, but feel free to use another type of bean or add tempeh or seitan instead of (or in addition to) the sausage. Like most soups and stews, this tastes even better the day after it's made.

1. Heat the water in a large saucepan over medium heat. Add the sausage and cook until browned, about 5 minutes, stirring occasionally. Remove the sausage from the pot and set aside.

2. Return the saucepan to medium heat and add the onion and ¼ cup (60 ml) of the broth. Cook for 5 minutes to soften, then add the lentils and remaining 2¾ (650 ml) cups of broth and bring to a boil.Reduce the heat to a simmer and cook for 15 minutes.

3. Stir in the potatoes, garlic, ginger, tomatoes, succotash, Worcestershire sauce, mustard, sugar, allspice, Tabasco, and salt and pepper to taste, and bring to a boil. Reduce the heat to low and cook until the lentils and vegetables are tender, about 45 minutes, stirring occasionally. During the last 10 minutes of cooking time, add the reserved sausage and the liquid smoke. Taste and adjust the seasonings, if needed.

Nutrition Analysis

Per serving [for 4]: 590 calories, 36 g protein, 7 g total fat, 103 g carbohydrate, 10 g sugar, 16 g fiber

Per serving [for 6]: 400 calories, 24 g protein, 4.5 g total fat, 69 g carbohydrate, 6 g sugar, 11 g fiber

Jambalaya Red Beans and Rice

Makes 4 servings

2 tablespoons (30 ml) water, or 1 tablespoon (15 ml) extra-virgin olive oil

4 to 6 Plant-Perfect Sausage links (page 170) or other vegan sausage links, cut into ½-inch [1 cm] slices

1 yellow onion, chopped

½ cup chopped celery

1 green bell pepper, seeded and chopped

3 garlic cloves, minced

½ cup (120 ml) water

3 tablespoons (48 g) tomato paste

1 (14.5-ounce [411 g]) can fire-roasted diced tomatoes with its juice

1 teaspoon dried thyme

1 teaspoon filé powder (optional)

½ teaspoon sea salt

¼ teaspoon cayenne

1½ cups (258 g) cooked dark red kidney beans or other red beans, or 1 (15-ounce [425 g]) can, rinsed and drained

3 cups (585 g) freshly cooked brown rice

1 teaspoon Tabasco sauce, plus more as needed

Red beans and rice combine with plant-based sausage and the culinary holy trinity of onion, green bell pepper, and celery for a satisfying and protein-rich taste of the New Orleans.

1. Heat the water in a large pot over medium heat. Add the sausage and cook until browned, about 5 minutes. Remove the sausage from the pot and set aside.

2. Return the pot to medium heat and add the onion, celery, bell pepper, and garlic. Add the water and cook, stirring occasionally, for 10 minutes, or until the vegetables begin to soften. Stir in the tomato paste, then add the tomatoes, thyme, filé powder, if using, salt, cayenne, and beans. Cover and simmer for 20 minutes, or until the vegetables and tender.

3. A few minutes before serving, stir in the rice, Tabasco, and the reserved sausage. Taste and adjust the seasonings, if needed. Serve hot.

Nutrition Analysis

Per serving: 500 calories, 33 g protein, 7 g total fat, 76 g carbohydrate, 7 g sugar, 14 g fiber

African Peanut Stew with Red Beans and Sweet Potatoes

Makes 4 servings

2 tablespoons (30 ml) water, or 1 tablespoon (15 ml) extra-virgin olive oil

1 yellow onion, chopped

1 red bell pepper, seeded and chopped

2 garlic cloves, minced

2 teaspoons grated fresh ginger

½ teaspoon ground cumin

¼ teaspoon cayenne, plus more to taste

1½ pounds (680 g) sweet potatoes, peeled and cut into ½-inch (1 cm) dice

1 (14.5-ounce [411 g]) can crushed tomatoes

2 cups (475 ml) vegetable broth

1 teaspoon sea salt, plus more if needed

3 cups (531 g) cooked dark red kidney beans, or 2 (15-ounce [425 g]) cans, rinsed and drained

3 tablespoons (48 g) creamy natural peanut butter

½ cup (75 g) chopped unsalted dry-roasted peanuts

This luscious stew is chock-full of vegetables, with extra plant protein coming from the dark red kidney beans and peanuts.

1. Heat the water in a large saucepan over medium heat. Add the onion, cover, and cook until softened, about 5 minutes. Add the bell pepper and garlic, cover, and cook until softened, about 5 minutes. Stir in the ginger, cumin, and cayenne and cook, stirring, for 30 seconds. Add the sweet potatoes and stir to coat. Stir in the tomatoes, broth, and salt. Bring to a boil, then reduce the heat to low, and simmer until the vegetables are soft, about 30 minutes.

2. About 10 minutes before the end of the cooking time, stir in the kidney beans and simmer until heated through.

3. Ladle ¼ cup (60 ml) of the broth into a small bowl. Add the peanut butter, stirring until smooth. Stir it into the stew. If a thicker consistency is desired, puree 1 cup (235 ml) of the stew in a blender or food processor and stir back into the pot. Taste and adjust the seasonings. Sprinkle with the chopped peanuts and serve.

Nutrition Analysis

Per serving: 520 calories, 23 g protein, 17 g total fat, 73 g carbohydrate, 17 g sugar, 18 g fiber

Spaghetti with Lentil Bolognese Sauce

Makes 4 servings

2 tablespoons (30 ml) water, or 1 tablespoon (15 ml) extra-virgin olive oil

1 yellow onion, minced

1 large carrot, minced

1 red bell pepper, seeded and minced

3 to 4 garlic cloves, minced

3 tablespoons (48 g) tomato paste

1 cup (192 g) red lentils, rinsed

3 cups (710 ml) water

Sea salt

2 tablespoons (8 g) nutritional yeast

2 teaspoons white miso paste

1 teaspoon dried basil

½ teaspoon dried oregano

½ teaspoon red pepper flakes, plus more if needed

1 teaspoon natural sugar

½ teaspoon freshly ground black pepper

1 (28-ounce [794 g]) jar marinara sauce, or 3½ cups homemade marinara sauce

¼ cup (60 ml) dry red wine or vegetable broth

½ cup (120 ml) Cashew Cream (page 178)

½ teaspoon liquid smoke

12 ounces (340 g) spaghetti

2 tablespoons (8 g) minced fresh parsley

Quick-cooking red lentils provide the protein in this flavorful Bolognese sauce that's made even richer with the addition of miso paste and nutritional yeast. I use spaghetti here because it is the traditional pasta served with Bolognese sauce, but feel free to use your favorite pasta. If you prefer the sauce less spicy, omit the red pepper flakes.

1. Heat the water in a large saucepan over medium heat. Add the onion, carrot, bell pepper, and garlic and cook, stirring occasionally, until softened, about 5 minutes. Stir in the tomato paste, lentils, water, and 1 teaspoon salt. Bring to a boil, then reduce the heat to a simmer and cook until the lentils and vegetables are tender, about 15 minutes.

2. Stir in the nutritional yeast, miso paste, basil, oregano, red pepper flakes, sugar, and black pepper. Add the marinara sauce and wine. Simmer until the sauce has thickened and the flavors have blended, about 10 minutes.

3. Stir in the cashew cream and liquid smoke. Taste and adjust the seasonings, if needed. Keep the sauce warm over low heat.

4. While the sauce is simmering, cook the spaghetti in a large pot of salted boiling water, stirring occasionally, until it is al dente, according to the package directions. Drain.

5. To serve, top the pasta with the sauce and serve hot sprinkled with fresh parsley.

Nutrition Analysis

Per serving: 680 calories, 29 g protein, 8 g total fat, 123 g carbohydrate, 19 g sugar, 11 g fiber

Edamame Fried Rice and Quinoa

Makes 4 servings

2 tablespoons (30 ml) water, or 1 tablespoon (15 ml) neutral-tasting vegetable oil, such as avocado oil

1 large yellow onion, chopped

2 garlic cloves, minced

1 carrot, shredded

1 small red bell pepper, seeded and chopped

2 cups (140 g) chopped bok choy

1¾ cups (341 g) cold cooked brown rice

¼ cups (324 g) cold cooked quinoa

1 cup (155 g) cooked shelled edamame

½ cup (65 g) frozen green peas, thawed

2 tablespoons (30 ml) tamari

1 teaspoon dark sesame oil (optional)

Sea salt and freshly ground black pepper

Take-out fried rice is a perennial favorite, but it can be loaded with oil and there's never enough vegetables. This recipe keeps the oil to a minimum while still retaining the flavor. Best of all, you can customize it to feature as many vegetables as you like. Use this recipe as a guide to create your own version, using whatever cooked grains you have on hand or vegetables you need to use up. To further increase the protein, you can add crumbled tofu or tempeh or chopped seitan.

1. Heat the water in a large nonstick skillet or wok over medium-high heat. Add the onion, garlic, and carrot, and stir-fry for 30 seconds. Add bell pepper and bok choy. Lower the heat to medium and stir-fry for 3 to 4 minutes to soften the vegetables, adding a little more water, if needed, so the vegetables don't burn.

2. Add the rice, quinoa, edamame, peas, tamari, sesame oil (if using), and salt and pepper to taste. Increase the heat to medium-high and stir-fry for 5 minutes more to heat through. Taste and adjust the seasonings, if needed. Serve hot.

Nutrition Analysis

Per serving: 290 calories, 13 g protein, 4.5 g total fat, 51 g carbohydrate, 6 g sugar, 8 g fiber

Pasta and White Beans with Spinach-Walnut Pesto

Makes 4 servings

3 cups lightly packed (90 g) baby spinach leaves

1 cup (24 g) fresh basil leaves, lightly packed

12 ounces (340 g) pasta

3 garlic cloves, crushed or coarsely chopped

⅓ cup (33 g) toasted walnut pieces

3 tablespoons (12 g) nutritional yeast

1 tablespoon (14 g) hulled hemp seeds

½ teaspoon salt, plus more if needed

¼ teaspoon freshly ground black pepper

2 tablespoons (30 ml) extra-virgin olive oil (optional)

1 tablespoon (15 ml) fresh lemon juice

1½ cups (266 g) cooked cannellini beans or other white beans, or 1 (15-ounce [425 g]) can, rinsed and drained

When you add spinach, walnut, and a few hemp seeds to your pesto, the protein content soars. Use a whole-grain or bean pasta and add some white beans, and you have a delicious and satisfying meal rich in plant protein. Leftover pesto can be stored in a small tightly covered container in the refrigerator for up to 3 days or in the freezer for up to 3 months.

1. Bring a large pot of water to the boil. Add the spinach and basil, pushing down to immerse them in the water, and blanch for about 1 minute, until just wilted. Drain the greens and transfer them to a bowl filled with ice water to cool and arrest the color. Drain the greens from the ice water and squeeze them to remove as much water as possible. Set aside.

2. Cook the pasta in a large pot of salted boiling water, stirring occasionally, until it is al dente, according to the package directions.

3. While the pasta is cooking, combine the garlic, toasted walnut pieces, nutritional yeast, hemp seeds, salt, and pepper in a food processor, and process until finely minced. Add the reserved spinach and basil and the olive oil (if using), and process to a paste. Add the lemon juice. Transfer ¼ cup (60 ml) of the hot pasta cooking water or more to the food processor and blend to achieve a desired consistency.

4. Put the beans in a colander in the sink. Drain, the pasta over the beans. Return the drained pasta and beans to the pot. Spoon on as much of the pesto as desired and toss gently to combine. Taste and adjust the seasonings, if needed. Serve hot.

Nutrition Analysis

Per serving: 510 calories, 23 g protein, 9 g total fat, 85 g carbohydrate, 4 g sugar, 7 g fiber

Indonesian Noodles with Tempeh

Makes 4 to 6 servings

8 ounces (225 g) rice vermicelli (or use cooked ramen or cooked spaghetti)

2 tablespoons (30 ml) water, or 1 tablespoon (15 ml) avocado oil

8 ounces (225 g) Braised Tempeh (page 167), cut into ½-inch [1 cm] dice

⅓ cup (70 ml) tamari

½ cup (130 g) creamy natural peanut butter

⅔ cup (140 ml) low-fat unsweetened coconut milk

2 tablespoons (30 ml) fresh lemon juice

1 to 2 teaspoons sambal oelek or other Asian chili paste (depending on how spicy you want it)

1 teaspoon natural sugar

1¼ cups (295 ml) water

1 red bell pepper, seeded and chopped

6 cups (420 g) chopped bok choy

1 large carrot, shredded

½ cup (50 g) chopped scallions, white and green parts

3 garlic cloves

1 tablespoon (8 g) grated fresh ginger

1 cup (134 g) frozen peas, thawed

¼ cup (35 g) chopped unsalted dry-roasted peanuts

2 tablespoons (8 g) minced fresh cilantro

Also known as bami goreng, these flavorful noodles are a popular dish in Indonesia. Tofu or seitan can be used instead of tempeh, if you prefer. Substitute rice for the noodles and you will have a dish called nasi goreng.

1. Soak the rice vermicelli in hot water until softened, about 5 minutes. Drain well, rinse, and set aside.

2. Heat the water in a large skillet or wok over medium-high heat. Add the tempeh and 1 tablespoon (15 ml) of the tamari and cook until the tempeh is browned on all sides. Remove the tempeh from the skillet and set aside.

3. In a food processor, combine the peanut butter, coconut milk, lemon juice, sambal oelek, sugar, and the remaining 4 tablespoons plus 1 teaspoon (64 ml) tamari. Add 1 cup (235 ml) of the water and process until smooth, then set aside.

4. Heat the remaining ¼ cup (60 ml) of water in a large skillet or wok over medium-high heat. Add the bell pepper, bok choy, carrot, scallions, garlic, and ginger and cook, stirring occasionally until softened, about 10 minutes.

5. Reduce the heat to low and stir in the peas and the reserved tempeh. Add the reserved noodles, stir in the sauce, and simmer until the noodles are hot and well coated with the sauce. Serve garnished with peanuts and cilantro.

Nutrition Analysis

Per serving [for 4]: 680 calories, 31 g protein, 31 g total fat, 73 g carbohydrate, 8 g sugar, 7 g fiber

Per serving [for 6]: 400 calories, 20 g protein, 20 g total fat, 49 g carbohydrate, 6 g sugar, 5 g fiber

Broccoli-Tofu Stir-Fry with Cashews

Makes 4 servings

3 cups (213 g) small broccoli florets

2 tablespoons (30 ml) tamari

2 tablespoons (32 g) almond butter

1 tablespoon (15 ml) rice vinegar

2 tablespoons (30 ml) hoisin sauce

½ teaspoon red pepper flakes

1 tablespoon (8 g) cornstarch

¾ cup (175 ml) water

1 red bell pepper, seeded and diced

1½ cups (105 g) sliced fresh shiitake mushroom caps

3 scallions, white and green parts, chopped

1 tablespoon (8 g) grated fresh ginger

2 garlic cloves, minced

Baked Marinated Tofu (page 176), cut into 1-inch [2.5 cm] dice

Freshly cooked rice, other grain, or noodles, to serve

½ cup (68 g) chopped roasted cashews

Tofu, broccoli, and cashews provide lots of protein and other nutrients in this delicious stir-fry. Prepare the tofu ahead of time, and the dish can be on the table in minutes. Instead of tofu, you can make this with tempeh or seitan, or simply add more (and different) vegetables. Serve over cooked rice or your favorite grain or toss with noodles.

1. Steam or blanch the broccoli until it turns bright green, about 1 minute. Drain, transfer to a bowl of ice water to stop the cooking process, and drain again. Set aside.

2. In a small bowl, combine the tamari, almond butter, vinegar, hoisin sauce, and red pepper flakes. Add the cornstarch and ¼ cup (60 ml) of the water, mix well, and set aside.

3. Heat the remaining ½ cup (120 ml) of water in a large skillet or wok over medium-high heat. Add the bell pepper, mushrooms, scallions, ginger, and garlic, and stir-fry for 1 minute. Add the reserved cornstarch mixture and stir to thicken the sauce. Add the tofu and broccoli and stir-fry to heat through and coat the tofu and broccoli with the sauce. Serve hot over cooked rice, topped with the cashews.

Nutrition Analysis

Per serving: 360 calories, 19 g protein, 18 g total fat, 36 g carbohydrate, 18 g sugar, 5 g fiber

Chapter 6
From the Oven

Plant-Powered Meat Loaf

Makes 6 servings

2 tablespoons (30 ml) water, or 1 tablespoon (15 ml) extra-virgin olive oil

1 large yellow onion, chopped

4 garlic cloves, minced

2 cups (140 g) chopped mushrooms (any type)

1 tablespoon (15 ml) tamari

1 tablespoon (16 g) tomato paste

¼ cup (15 g) chopped fresh parsley

1 cup (156 g) old-fashioned rolled oats

½ cup (50 g) walnuts pieces

½ cup (73 g) sunflower seed kernels

2 tablespoons (16 g) cornstarch or tapioca starch

1 teaspoon dried thyme

½ teaspoon ground sage

1 teaspoon sea salt

¼ teaspoon freshly ground black pepper

3 cups (594 g) cooked brown lentils or dark red kidney beans, or 2 (15-ounce [425 g]) cans, rinsed and well drained, mashed

2 cups (390 g) cooked brown rice, quinoa, or other grain, cooled

Nutrition Analysis
Per serving: 400 calories, 17 g protein, 15 g total fat, 55 g carbohydrate, 5 g sugar, 13 g fiber

Lentils and brown rice (or your choice of beans and grains) combine with oats, nuts, and seasonings to make a delicious no-meat loaf. Top it with the optional glaze or serve it with the brown gravy on page 122. Leftovers make great sandwiches.

1. Preheat the oven to 350°F (180°C). Lightly oil a 9 by 5-inch (23 by 13 cm) loaf pan or line it with parchment paper. Set aside.

2. Heat the water in a large skillet over medium heat. Add the onion and cook until softened, about 5 minutes. Add the garlic and mushrooms and cook until softened, stirring occasionally, about 5 minutes more. Stir in the tamari, tomato paste, and parsley and set aside to cool.

3. In a food processor, combine the oats, walnuts, and sunflower seeds and process until finely ground. Add the cornstarch, thyme, sage, salt, and pepper and pulse to mix.

4. Add the mashed lentils and rice to the onion mixture, then add the oat mixture and mix well to combine thoroughly. Transfer the mixture to the prepared pan and press the mixture evenly and firmly into the pan, smoothing the top. Cover with foil and bake for 40 minutes, then uncover and bake for another 10 minutes to brown the top. Remove from the oven and let it stand for about 10 minutes to firm up.

5. To serve, carefully loosen the edges of the loaf with a knife, if necessary, and invert onto a serving platter. Use a long serrated knife to slice.

Optional Glaze: In a small bowl, combine ½ cup (120 g) ketchup with 3 tablespoons (45 g) natural sugar and 1 tablespoon (15 ml) cider vinegar. Mix well, then spread the glaze mixture evenly on top of the loaf before baking.

Nutrition Analysis
Glaze per serving: 50 calories, 0 g protein, 0 g total fat, 13 g carbohydrate, 11 g sugar, 0 g fiber

Easy Peasy
Mac & Cheesy

Makes 4 to 6 servings

16 ounces (455 g) elbow macaroni or other small pasta

1 cup (30 g) raw cashews, soaked in hot water for 30 minutes, then drained

1 (12-ounce [340 g]) package silken tofu, drained

2 cups (475 ml) plain unsweetened plant milk

½ cup (32 g) nutritional yeast

2 tablespoons (30 ml) tamari

2 teaspoons prepared yellow mustard

1 teaspoon onion powder

1 teaspoon garlic powder

1 teaspoon smoked paprika, plus more to garnish

1 teaspoon sea salt

1½ cups (201 g) frozen green peas, thawed

½ cup (40 g) ground toasted walnuts

Cleverly disguised as delicious comfort food, this mac and cheese is a protein powerhouse thanks to ingredients such as tofu, cashews, green peas, and walnuts. Nutritional yeast lends even more protein and a cheesy flavor. For even more protein, use a bean-based pasta (just be sure not to overcook it!).

1. Preheat the oven to 350°F (180°C). Lightly oil a 9 by 13-inch (33 by 23 cm) baking dish and set it aside.

2. Bring a large pot of salted water to a boil over high heat. Add the pasta and cook according to the package directions until al dente. Reserve 1 cup (235 ml) of the pasta cooking water. Drain the pasta and transfer it to the prepared baking dish.

3. In a high-speed blender, combine the cashews and reserved cooking water, tofu, plant milk, nutritional yeast, tamari, mustard, onion powder, garlic powder, paprika, and salt. Blend until completely smooth. Pour the cheese sauce over the pasta, add the peas, and stir gently to combine. Sprinkle the top with the ground toasted walnuts and lightly sprinkle with more paprika.

4. Cover the baking dish with aluminum foil and bake for 20 minutes. Serve hot.

Nutrition Analysis

Per serving: 440 calories, 20 g protein, 11 g total fat, 67 g carbohydrate, 5 g sugar, 4 g fiber

White Bean Cassoulet

Makes 4 servings

2 tablespoons (30 ml) water, or 1 tablespoon (15 ml) extra-virgin olive oil

1 large yellow onion, chopped

2 large carrots, thinly sliced

3 garlic cloves, minced

1 tablespoon (15 ml) tamari

1 tablespoon (16 g) tomato paste

2 teaspoons Dijon mustard

1 teaspoon dried thyme

1 teaspoon dried marjoram

½ teaspoon smoked paprika

1 bay leaf

½ teaspoon sea salt

¼ teaspoon freshly ground black pepper

1 tablespoon (16 g) white or chickpea miso paste

¾ cup (175 ml) water

3 cups (531 g) cooked great Northern beans, or 2 (15-ounce [425 g]) cans, drained and rinsed

1½ cups (265 g) cooked cannellini beans, or 1 (15-ounce [425 g]) can, drained and rinsed

1 (14.5-ounce [411 g]) can diced fire-roasted tomatoes with its juice

1 teaspoon liquid smoke

2 tablespoons (8 g) chopped fresh parsley

This classic country French stew is traditionally baked for several hours in the oven, but with this plant-based version, the cooking time is shortened. It can also be made on a stovetop or in a slow cooker. My version features two kinds of white beans, but you can add two or three plant-based sausage links if you like—simply slice and pan-fry the sausage and then add to the cassoulet when you are ready to serve so they retain their texture.

1. Preheat the oven to 350°F (180°C). Lightly oil a large casserole dish and set it aside.

2. Heat the 2 tablespoons (30 ml) water in a large skillet over medium heat. Add the onion and carrots and cook until softened, about 5 minutes. Stir in the garlic and cook, stirring, until fragrant, about 30 seconds. Stir in the tamari, tomato paste, and mustard. Add the thyme, marjoram, paprika, bay leaf, salt, and pepper. Stir in the miso paste and the ¾ cup (175 ml) water, then remove from the heat.

3. Combine all the beans, the tomatoes and their juice, and liquid smoke in the prepared casserole dish. Add the sautéed vegetable mixture and stir to mix well. Cover tightly and bake until the vegetables are tender and the flavors are well blended, about 45 minutes.

4. Taste and adjust the seasonings, if needed. Remove the bay leaf before serving. Serve hot sprinkled with the parsley.

Nutrition Analysis

Per serving: 320 calories, 20 g protein, 1 g total fat, 60 g carbohydrate, 8 g sugar, 18 g fiber

PROTEIN PLUS

Super Shepherd's Pie

Makes 6 servings

2 tablespoons water (30 ml), or 1 tablespoon (15 ml) extra-virgin olive oil

1 yellow onion, chopped

2 carrots, chopped

8 ounces (225 g) white button mushrooms, chopped

½ teaspoon onion powder

½ teaspoon dried thyme

Sea salt and freshly ground black pepper

2 cups (396 g) cooked or canned brown lentils, drained

1 cup (134 g) fresh or thawed frozen peas

1 cup (164 g) fresh or thawed frozen corn kernels

2 tablespoons (8 g) nutritional yeast

3 cups (710 ml) Almost-Instant Brown Gravy (page 122)

3½ cups (828 ml) White Bean Mashed Potatoes (page 121)

¼ teaspoon smoked paprika

This cozy casserole features cooked lentils in place of the ground meat, but you can also use chopped seitan, tempeh, or reconstituted TVP, if you prefer.

1. Preheat the oven to 375°F (190°C). Lightly oil a 9 by 13-inch (23 by 33 cm) baking dish or coat with cooking spray.
2. Heat the water in a large skillet over medium heat. Add the onion and carrots and cook until tender, about 5 minutes. Add the mushrooms, onion powder, and thyme. Cook, stirring occasionally, for 4 minutes to soften the mushrooms. Season with salt and pepper to taste. Remove from the heat and stir in the lentils, peas, corn, and nutritional yeast. Add the gravy, stirring to combine. Taste and adjust the seasonings, if needed.
3. Spoon the mixture into the prepared baking dish. Spread the mashed potatoes over the top. Sprinkle with the paprika. Bake until the filling is hot and bubbly and the potatoes are golden on top, 35 to 45 minutes. Serve hot.

Nutrition Analysis

Per serving: 340 calories, 20 g protein, 1 g total fat, 65 g carbohydrate, 9 g sugar, 18 g fiber

White Bean Mashed Potatoes

Makes about 3½ cups (788 g)

1½ pounds (680 g) Yukon gold or russet potatoes, peeled and cut into 2-inch (5 cm) chunks

1 cup (256 g) cooked or canned cannellini or other white beans, rinsed and drained

½ cup (120 ml) vegetable broth

3 tablespoons (12 g) nutritional yeast

½ teaspoon garlic powder

½ teaspoon sea salt, plus more if needed

The addition of pureed white beans and nutritional yeast significantly increases the protein (and flavor!) in these mashed potatoes. In addition to making a great topper for the Shepherd's Pie, it also makes a tasty main dish when topped with roasted or sautéed vegetables and some brown gravy.

1. Cover the potatoes with cold salted water in a large pot. Bring to a boil over medium-high heat and cook until the potatoes are tender when pierced with a fork, about 20 minutes.

2. While the potatoes are cooking, combine the white beans, vegetable broth, nutritional yeast, and garlic powder in a blender or food processor and blend until smooth. Set aside.

3. Drain the potatoes, return them to the pot, and mash with a potato masher. Add the reserved white bean mixture and salt to taste. Mash until all of the ingredients are well mixed and the potatoes are smooth. Taste and adjust the seasonings, if needed.

Nutrition Analysis

Per ½-cup (113 g) serving: 110 calories, 5 g protein, 0 g total fat, 23 g carbohydrate, 1 g sugar, 5 g fiber

Almost-Instant Brown Gravy

Makes about 3 cups (710 ml)

1 cup (70 g) chopped mushrooms (any type)

1 (15-ounce [425 g]) can cannellini or other white beans, rinsed and drained

¼ cup (16 g) nutritional yeast

1¼ cups (295 ml) vegetable broth

1 teaspoon onion powder

½ teaspoon garlic powder

½ teaspoon dried thyme

¼ teaspoon ground coriander

¼ teaspoon smoked paprika

2 tablespoons (30 ml) tamari

1 teaspoon browning liquid (Kitchen Bouquet or Gravy Master)

Sea salt and freshly ground black pepper

This quick and easy gravy is so delicious, you'll want to spoon it over everything from veggie burgers to no-meat loaf. It's especially good in the Super Shepherd's Pie (page 118).

1. In a heatproof bowl, microwave the mushrooms for a minute to soften. Drain the mushrooms and transfer to a blender or food processor. Add the white beans, nutritional yeast, and ½ cup (120 ml) of the broth and blend until smooth. Add the onion powder, garlic powder, thyme, coriander, paprika, tamari, browning liquid, and remaining ½ cup (120 ml) of broth. Blend until smooth. Taste and adjust the seasonings, adding salt and pepper to taste.

2. If using in the shepherd's pie, you can add it to the vegetables at this point. If using as a sauce for other recipes, transfer the gravy to a small saucepan and heat before serving. If not using right away, transfer to a container with a tight lid, cover, and refrigerate for up to 3 days.

Nutrition Analysis

Per ¼-cup (60 ml) serving: 35 calories, 3 g protein, 0 g total fat, 5 g carbohydrate, 1 g sugar, 2 g fiber

Chili-Cheesy Baked Potatoes

Makes 4 servings

4 russet potatoes, well-scrubbed and dried

½ cup (120 ml) Cashew Sour Cream (page 180) or store-bought vegan sour cream

2 scallions, white and green parts, minced

½ teaspoon sea salt

¼ teaspoon freshly ground black pepper

2 cups (475 ml) Three-Bean Chili (page 97) or other vegan chili, warmed

1 cup (235 ml) Easy Cheesy Sauce (page 44), warmed

These baked potatoes topped with hearty chili and drizzled with a cheesy sauce make a simple meal that's simply fantastic when served with a green salad. Bonus: It's a great way to use up leftover chili.

1. Preheat the oven to 400°F (200°C). Line a rimmed baking sheet with parchment paper or a silicone mat and set aside.

2. Pierce the potatoes in several places with a fork. Arrange the potatoes directly on the center rack of the oven and bake until tender, 50 to 60 minutes. Remove the potatoes from the oven and set aside for 10 minutes, or until cool enough to handle.

3. Cut the baked potatoes in half lengthwise and scoop the insides into a bowl, leaving about ¼ inch (6 mm) of the potato with the skin so they're sturdy enough to stuff. To the bowl, add the sour cream, scallions, salt, and pepper and mash well to combine.

4. Fill the potato skins evenly with the potato mixture and arrange them on the prepared baking sheet. Bake for 15 minutes, until hot.

5. To serve, arrange the baked potato halves on plates (two halves per serving). Spoon the warm chili onto the potatoes, then drizzle the warm cheesy sauce on top of the chili and serve.

Nutrition Analysis

Per serving: 340 calories, 13 g protein, 7 g total fat, 60 g carbohydrate, 7 g sugar, 10 g fiber

Roasted Cauliflower and Potatoes with Chickpeas and Charmoula Sauce

1 large head cauliflower, core and leaves removed

16 ounces (455g) small baby potatoes, scrubbed and quartered

Sea salt and freshly ground black pepper

1½ cups (246 g) cooked chickpeas, or 1 (15-ounce [425 g]) can, drained and rinsed

¾ packed cup (45 g) coarsely chopped fresh parsley

¾ packed cup (45 g) coarsely chopped fresh cilantro

1 garlic clove, minced

¼ cup (64 g) almond butter

¼ cup (60 ml) extra-virgin olive oil

1 tablespoon (15 ml) fresh lemon juice

1 tablespoon (15 ml) red wine vinegar

2 teaspoons nutritional yeast

1 teaspoon smoked paprika

¼ teaspoon ground cumin

¼ teaspoon ground coriander

¼ teaspoon red pepper flakes, plus more if needed

Charmoula sauce, kind of a North African pesto, is a delicious topping for tender roasted cauliflower and potatoes in this sheet pan supper.

1. Preheat the oven to 425°F (220°C). Line one or two large rimmed baking sheets with parchment paper or coat with cooking spray.

2. On a cutting board, cored-side down, use a serrated knife to cut the cauliflower into ½-inch (1 cm) slices, as if you were cutting a loaf of bread. It's okay if some of the cauliflower slices fall apart. Arrange the cauliflower and potatoes on the prepared baking sheets and spray the vegetables with cooking spray. Season with salt and pepper to taste.

3. Roast the cauliflower and potatoes for 15 minutes, then remove from the oven and turn over the pieces with a large metal spatula. Scatter the chickpeas on and around the cauliflower and potatoes. Return the pan to the oven and continue roasting until the cauliflower and potatoes are tender and nicely browned, 10 to 15 minutes longer.

4. While the vegetables are roasting, make the sauce. In a food processor, combine the parsley, cilantro, garlic, almond butter, olive oil, lemon juice, vinegar, nutritional yeast, paprika, cumin, coriander, and red pepper flakes. Process until well blended. Taste and add more red pepper flakes, if desired.

5. When the vegetables are tender, transfer them to a platter or shallow serving bowl and spoon the charmoula sauce on top. Serve hot.

Nutrition Analysis

Per serving: 470 calories, 16 g protein, 26 g total fat, 51 g carbohydrate, 10 g sugar, 14 g fiber

Sheet Pan Provençale Vegetables

1 yellow onion, diced

1 eggplant, peeled and diced

2 or 3 zucchini, diced

1 large red bell pepper, seeded and diced

1 large yellow bell pepper, seeded and diced

3 garlic cloves, coarsely chopped

1 (14.5-ounce [411 g]) can fire-roasted diced tomatoes with its juice

1½ cups (266 g) cooked cannellini or other white beans, or 1 (15-ounce [425 g]) can, drained and rinsed

½ teaspoon sea salt, plus more if needed

¼ teaspoon freshly ground black pepper

1 teaspoon dried marjoram

1 teaspoon dried thyme

Cooked pasta or your favorite grain, to serve

2 tablespoons (8 g) minced fresh parsley

The traditional French vegetable stew known as ratatouille gets an update as a sheet pan supper. Roasting brings out the flavor of the vegetables and white beans add protein. Serve alone as a side dish or spoon over cooked pasta or your favorite grain and make it a meal.

1. Preheat the oven to 425°F (220°C). Line two rimmed baking sheets with parchment paper or coat with cooking spray.

2. Spread the onion, eggplant, zucchini, bell peppers, and garlic in a single layer on the pans. Coat the vegetables lightly with cooking spray and season with salt and pepper. Roast the vegetables for 15 minutes. Remove from the oven and stir the tomatoes and white beans into the vegetables. Sprinkle with the marjoram and thyme, and add more salt and pepper, if needed. Return the pans to the oven and roast until the vegetables are tender, 10 to 15 minutes longer.

3. Stir in the parsley. Taste and the adjust seasonings, if necessary. Serve immediately over cooked pasta or your favorite grain and sprinkle with fresh parsley.

Nutrition Analysis

Per serving (not including pasta or grain): 200 calories, 11 g protein, 1 g total fat, 40 g carbohydrate, 11 g sugar, 12 g fiber

PROTEIN PLUS

Major Lasagna

1½ cups (266 g) cooked cannellini beans, or 1 (15-ounce [425 g]) can, drained and rinsed

1 (16-ounce [455 g]) container firm tofu, well drained

1 (12-ounce [340 g]) package silken tofu, drained

10 ounces (280 g) fresh spinach, blanched, or frozen spinach, thawed, chopped

⅓ cup (21 g) nutritional yeast

1 tablespoon (15 ml) fresh lemon juice

1 teaspoon onion powder

1 teaspoon garlic powder

1 teaspoon dried basil

1 teaspoon dried oregano

1 teaspoon sea salt, plus more if needed

½ teaspoon freshly ground black pepper, plus more if needed

4 cups (946 ml) marinara sauce

½ cup (120 ml) water (optional)

1 (8 to 10-ounce [225 to 280 g]) box regular or no-boil vegan lasagna noodles (see Note)

Little Lentil Balls (page 46) or other vegan meatballs, cooked (optional)

½ cup (120 ml) Protein Parm (page 129)

You can assemble the lasagna up to 2 days ahead of baking it. Tightly wrap the baking dish in plastic and refrigerate it. Let the lasagna come to room temperature before baking.

1. Mash the beans in a bowl or process to a puree in a food processor. Add both kinds of tofu and mash well or pulse to combine. Add the nutritional yeast, lemon juice, onion powder, garlic powder, basil, oregano, salt, and pepper. Mash or pulse until well mixed. Don't overmix. Taste and adjust the seasonings, if needed. Set aside.

2. Preheat the oven to 375°F (190°C).

3. Spread 1 cup (235 ml) of the marinara sauce in the bottom of a 9 by 13 inch (23 by 33 cm) baking dish. (Note: If you do not precook your noodles, stir about ½ cup [120 ml] water into this bottom layer of sauce.) Arrange a layer of noodles on top of the sauce. Evenly spread about half of the tofu mixture over the noodles. Arrange another layer of noodles on top of the tofu and spread a layer of marinara sauce over the noodles. Repeat the layers with the remaining noodles, ricotta mixture, and marinara sauce, ending with the lentil balls, if using, and the remaining sauce. Be sure to cover the lentil balls with sauce so they don't dry out. Sprinkle the Protein Parm on top of the marinara sauce.

4. Cover the baking dish tightly with aluminum foil and bake for 45 to 60 minutes, or until the noodles are tender. (The baking time may take a little longer if you used regular, not-parboiled noodles.) Let the lasagna cool for 10 minutes before serving.

Nutrition Analysis

Per serving: 360 calories, 20 g protein, 11 g total fat, 46 g carbohydrate, 8 g sugar, 6 g fiber

Protein Parm

Makes about 1 cup (128 g)

½ cup (55 g) slivered almonds

½ cup (50 g) walnut pieces

¼ cup (16 g) nutritional yeast

1 tablespoon (7 g) hulled hemp seeds

¾ teaspoon sea salt

This is an easy and tasty alternative to parmesan cheese. Use it as a topping on pasta dishes, salads, or anywhere else you want a salty, cheesy flavor.

1. Combine all the ingredients in a food processor and process until finely ground.

2. Transfer to a covered container or shaker and keep refrigerated for up to a month.

Nutrition Analysis

Per 2 tablespoon (10 g) serving: 100 calories, 4 g protein, 9 g total fat, 3 g carbohydrate, 1 g sugar, 2 g fiber

Note:

You can use your choice of oven-ready or regular vegan lasagna noodles to make this lasagna (the variation in weight of box is based on different brands). You can parboil regular noodles or not. When using oven-ready noodles (or regular noodles that are not parboiled), I add about ½ cup (120 ml) of water to the bottom of the baking dish (stirred into the bottom layer of marinara sauce) for the noodles to absorb as they cook.

PROTEIN PLUS

Black Bean Enchiladas

1½ cups (266 g) cooked black beans, or 1 (15-ounce [425 g]) can, drained and rinsed

2 teaspoons mild chili powder

½ teaspoon onion powder

1 cup (164 g) fresh or thawed frozen corn kernels

2 tablespoons (30 ml) water, or 1 tablespoon (15 ml) neutral-tasting vegetable oil, such as avocado oil

1 yellow onion, finely chopped

3 garlic cloves, minced

2 cups (140 g) chopped mushrooms (any type)

1 teaspoon dried oregano

1 teaspoon ground coriander

½ teaspoon ground cumin

Sea salt and freshly ground black pepper

6 cups (180 g) fresh baby spinach

1 (24-ounce [680 g]) jar tomato-based salsa

8 (9-inch [23 cm]) sprouted whole-grain tortillas

1 cup (235 ml) Easy Cheesy Sauce (page 44)

½ cup (114 g) toasted, salted pumpkin seed kernels (pepitas)

Loaded with good-for-you ingredients such as spinach, mushrooms, corn, and black beans, these super-tasty enchiladas are liberally doused with tomato salsa, then drizzled with a cheesy sauce, and sprinkled with toasted pepitas. That's a whole lot of yum!

1. Combine the black beans, 1 teaspoon of the chili powder, and the onion powder in a bowl and mash well. Fold in the corn kernels and set aside.

2. Preheat the oven to 350°F (180°C).

3. Heat the water in a saucepan over medium-high heat. Add the onion, garlic, mushrooms, oregano, coriander, cumin, remaining 1 teaspoon of chili powder, and salt and pepper to taste. Cook, stirring, until the onion is softened, about 5 minutes. Add the spinach and cook, stirring, until the spinach is wilted. Remove from the heat and set aside.

4. Pour about half of the salsa into a 9 by 13-inch (23 by 33 cm) baking dish and spread it evenly to cover the bottom of the dish. Spread about ¼ cup (60 ml) of the black bean mixture down one side of a tortilla. Top with about ⅓ cup (70 ml) of the mushroom mixture. Roll the tortilla up and around the filling and place in the baking dish, seam-side down, on top of the salsa. Repeat this with the remaining tortillas and filling. Pour the remaining salsa over top of the enchiladas, spreading evenly. Drizzle the Cheesy Sauce evenly over top and sprinkle with the pepitas.

5. Bake the enchiladas until heated through, about 20 minutes. Serve hot.

Nutrition Analysis

Per serving [for 4]: 660 calories, 33 g protein, 19 g total fat, 100 g carbohydrate, 12 g sugar, 26 g fiber

Per serving [for 6]: 440 calories, 22 g protein, 13 g total fat, 67 g carbohydrate, 8 g sugar, 17 g fiber

Chickpea Piccata with Mushrooms

Makes 4 servings

Cutlets

1½ cups (246 g) cooked chickpeas, or 1 (15-ounce [425 g]) can, drained, rinsed, and blotted dry

2 tablespoons (20 ml) tamari

¾ cup (108 g) vital wheat gluten

2 tablespoons (16 g) nutritional yeast

½ teaspoon onion powder

½ teaspoon garlic powder

½ teaspoon sweet paprika

¼ teaspoon sea salt

1 tablespoon (15 ml) extra-virgin olive oil

1 cup (235 ml) water

Mushrooms and Piccata Sauce

1½ cups (105 g) sliced mushrooms (any type)

Water

Sea salt and freshly ground black pepper

1 tablespoon (16 g) almond butter

⅓ cup (70 ml) vegetable broth

¼ cup (60 ml) dry white wine

2 tablespoons (30 ml) fresh lemon juice

1 tablespoon (9 g) capers

2 tablespoons (8 g) minced fresh parsley

1 tablespoon (15 ml) vegan butter

Try these lemon-kissed cutlets the next time you want to make something special for dinner. I like to serve them with White Bean Mashed Potatoes (page 121) and roasted asparagus.

1. Preheat the oven to 275°F (140°C).

2. In a food processor, combine the chickpeas and tamari and process until smooth. Add the vital wheat gluten, nutritional yeast, onion powder, garlic powder, paprika, and salt. Pulse until well mixed.

3. Transfer the mixture onto a work surface and knead with your hands for 1 to 2 minutes to fully incorporate. Divide the mixture into eight equal pieces and shape them into ¼-inch (6 mm) thick patties.

4. Heat the olive oil in a large skillet over medium heat. Add the patties, in batches if needed, and cook until golden brown, about 5 minutes per side. Reduce the heat to low, add the water to the skillet, cover, and cook for 10 minutes, in batches with additional water if needed, for 10 to 15 minutes; they should be firm to the touch. Remove the patties from the skillet (do not wash) and place them on a rimmed baking sheet. Place them in the oven while you make the sauce.

5. To make the sauce, add the mushrooms to the same skillet over medium heat and cook, stirring, until the mushrooms are tender, adding about 1 tablespoon (15 ml) of water so the mushrooms don't burn. Season with salt and pepper to taste. Remove the mushrooms from the skillet and set aside.

(Continued)

(Continued)

6. To make the sauce, add the mushrooms to the same skillet over medium heat and cook, stirring, until the mushrooms are tender, adding about 1 tablespoon (15 ml) of water so the mushrooms don't burn. Season with salt and pepper to taste. Remove the mushrooms from the skillet and set aside.

7. In the same skillet over medium heat, combine the almond butter and vegetable broth and cook, stirring to blend. Add the wine, lemon juice, capers, and parsley. Season with salt and pepper to taste. Simmer until the sauce thickens a little, about 3 minutes. Add the butter, stirring until melted. Return the mushrooms to the skillet and cook for a minute to heat through. To serve, transfer the cutlets to a serving platter and drizzle with the sauce and mushrooms.

Nutrition Analysis

Per serving: 320 calories, 29 g protein, 11 g total fat, 26 g carbohydrate, 4 g sugar, 6 g fiber

Chapter 7
Breakfasts of Champions

Super Frittata

Makes 2 servings

2 tablespoons (30 ml) water, or 1 tablespoon (15 ml) extra-virgin olive oil

½ cup (80 g) minced red onion

1 red bell pepper, seeded and finely chopped

1 link Plant-Perfect Sausage (page 170), finely chopped (or other vegan sausage)

Sea salt and freshly ground black pepper

12 to 16 ounces (340 to 455 g) firm tofu, drained

½ cup (43 g) chickpea flour

½ cup (120 ml) soy milk or other plant milk

3 tablespoons (12 g) nutritional yeast

2 teaspoons fresh lemon juice

½ teaspoon baking powder

½ teaspoon onion powder

½ teaspoon garlic powder

½ teaspoon ground turmeric

½ teaspoon fine kala namak (black salt) (optional)

2 tablespoons (8 g) minced fresh parsley, to serve

1 tablespoon (5 g) Protein Parm (page 129), to serve

Super easy. Super delicious. Super loaded with protein. Is it any wonder I call this is a super frittata? Best of all, it's extremely versatile: add more veggies (try mushrooms, kale, asparagus, or zucchini) or add some chopped tempeh bacon or vegan cheese for even more protein.

1. Preheat the oven to 350°F (180°C). Lightly coat an ovenproof skillet or round shallow baking dish or pie plate with cooking oil spray.

2. Heat the water in a skillet over medium-high heat. Add the onion, bell pepper, and sausage and cook for 5 minutes, or until the vegetables are tender. Season with salt and pepper to taste. Remove from the heat and set aside.

3. In a blender or food processor, combine the tofu, chickpea flour, soy milk, nutritional yeast, lemon juice, baking powder, onion powder, garlic powder, turmeric, kala namak, if using, and salt and pepper to taste. Blend until smooth.

4. Combine the reserved cooked vegetables and sausage with the tofu mixture and spread it evenly in the prepared skillet or baking dish.

5. Bake for 30 minutes, or until the frittata is golden brown and nicely set.

6. Let the frittata sit for 10 minutes. Sprinkle with parsley and Protein Parm, cut into wedges, and serve.

Nutrition Analysis

Per serving (12 ounces [340 g] tofu): 430 calories, 37 g protein, 15 g total fat, 37 g carbohydrate, 8 g sugar, 8 g fiber

Per serving (16 ounces [455 g] tofu): 480 calories, 42 g protein, 18 g total fat, 39 g carbohydrate, 8 g sugar, 8 g fiber

Cookies for Breakfast

1 cup (156 g) old-fashioned rolled oats

½ cup (46 g) oat flour

½ cup (60 g) dried blueberries, cranberries, or goji berries

½ cup (60 g) chopped toasted walnuts or pecans

¼ cup (28 g) ground golden flaxseeds

1 tablespoon (11 g) ground chia seeds

¾ teaspoon ground ginger or cinnamon

½ teaspoon baking powder

¼ teaspoon sea salt

1 ripe banana, mashed

¼ cup (80 g) pure maple syrup

2 tablespoons (30 ml) neutral-tasting vegetable oil, such as avocado oil

3 tablespoons (45 ml) plain unsweetened plant milk

1 teaspoon pure vanilla extract

Loaded with protein and bursting with flavorful and healthful ingredients, these not-too-sweet cookies are perfect for breakfast-on-the go.

1. Preheat the oven to 325°F (163°C). Line a rimmed baking sheet with parchment paper or coat lightly with cooking spray.

2. In a large bowl, combine the oats, oat flour, dried blueberries, walnuts, ground flaxseeds, chia seeds, ginger, baking powder, and salt. Stir in the mashed banana, maple syrup, oil, plant milk, and vanilla until well blended. Set aside for 4 minutes to set.

3. Scoop out about ¼ cup (60 ml) of the dough and place it on the baking sheet. Repeat with the remaining dough, spacing them about 2 inches (5 cm) apart. Gently press the dough with the palm of your hand to flatten slightly.

4. Bake for 15 minutes, until the cookies are lightly golden. Cool on wire racks. When completely cool, store the cookies in an airtight container in the refrigerator for up to 1 week.

Nutrition Analysis

Per cookie: 180 calories, 4 g protein, 9 g total fat, 23 g carbohydrate, 11 g sugar, 3 g fiber

Sausage and Sweet Potato Hash

Makes 4 servings

2 large sweet potatoes, peeled and diced

½ teaspoon onion powder

Sea salt and freshly ground black pepper

2 tablespoons (30 ml) water, or 1 tablespoon (15 ml) extra-virgin olive oil

½ cup (80 g) chopped yellow onion

2 garlic cloves, minced

2 Plant-Perfect Sausage links (page 170) or store-bought vegan sausage, chopped

½ cup (67 g) frozen green peas, thawed

2 scallions, white and green parts, minced

I prefer to make diced roasted sweet potatoes for this recipe because they hold their shape, but the recipe also works with leftover baked sweet potatoes (or white potatoes, for that matter) if you have them on hand. Just skip the roasting step and start on step 4. This hearty hash is great served any time of day.

1. Preheat the oven to 425° F (220°F). Line a rimmed baking sheet with parchment paper or lightly coat with cooking spray.

2. Spread the diced sweet potatoes in a single layer on the baking sheet. Spray the sweet potatoes with a little cooking spray and season with onion powder and salt and pepper.

3. Roast until tender and lightly browned, 20 to 25 minutes. Remove from the oven and set aside to cool.

4. Heat the water in large skillet over medium heat. Add the onion and garlic and cook until softened, about 5 minutes. Add the sausage, green peas, scallions, 1 teaspoon salt, and ½ teaspoon black pepper. Stir to combine and cook for 5 minutes. Add the reserved sweet potatoes, and cook for 5 to 10 minutes, stirring occasionally, until the potatoes and sausage are lightly browned. Serve hot.

Nutrition Analysis

Per serving: 200 calories, 14 g protein, 3 g total fat, 31 g carbohydrate, 8 g sugar, 6 g fiber

Potato and Bacon Breakfast Burritos

Makes 2 servings

8 ounces (225 g) firm tofu, drained and crumbled

½ teaspoon onion powder

½ teaspoon chili powder

½ teaspoon ground turmeric

½ teaspoon sea salt

1 baked russet potato, diced

¼ cup (60 ml) canned hot or mild diced green chiles, drained

4 slices Tempeh Bacon (page 173) or store-bought vegan bacon, chopped

½ cup (120 ml) tomato-based salsa, hot or mild

2 tablespoons (8 g) chopped fresh cilantro (optional)

2 large sprouted grain tortillas or flour tortillas

⅓ cup (70 ml) Easy Cheesy Sauce (page 44)

When you bake potatoes, make extra so you have some on hand for recipes like this one. If you don't have any on hand, dice a raw potato and steam it for 5 minutes or until tender.

1. Lightly coat a large skillet with cooking spray and heat over medium heat. Add the tofu, onion powder, chili powder, turmeric, and salt and cook, stirring and mashing to break up the tofu until the tofu is hot and the ingredients are well combined, about 4 minutes. Add the diced baked potato, green chiles, and bacon. Cook, stirring to mix well and heat through, about 2 minutes. Add the salsa and cilantro, if using, and cook for 1 minute more. Keep warm.

2. Heat a large dry skillet over medium-high heat. Add the tortillas, one at a time, and warm until they soften. Transfer the tortillas to a flat work surface. Spoon a thin line of the cheesy sauce down the center of each tortilla to within 1 inch (2.5 cm) from the edge. Arrange the tofu mixture on top of the sauce on each tortilla. Fold in the top and bottom of each tortilla and roll from one side to seal up the burrito.

3. Place one burrito, seam-side down, in the hot dry skillet for 1 minute, or until it becomes golden. Rotate the burrito until it is golden all over. Repeat with remaining burrito. Serve hot.

Nutrition Analysis

Per serving: 500 calories, 26 g protein, 17 g total fat, 64 g carbohydrate, 12 g sugar, 10 g fiber

Banana–Peanut Butter Overnight Oats

1 ripe banana, mashed

3 tablespoons (48 g) natural creamy peanut butter

2 tablespoons (22 g) chia seeds

¼ teaspoon ground cinnamon

1 cup (156 g) old-fashioned rolled oats

1¼ cups (295 ml) plain unsweetened plant milk

1 tablespoon (20 g) pure maple syrup

⅛ teaspoon sea salt

2 tablespoons (14 g) crushed toasted pecans

Optional toppings: dried cranberries, ground golden flaxseeds, fresh or thawed frozen blueberries, hulled hemp seeds

Soaking the oatmeal mixture overnight cuts down on morning prep time. Grab and go or heat and eat (depending on if you prefer your oatmeal cold or hot). This recipe makes enough for two or three, or just yourself, for a few days in a row.

1. The night before, mash the banana, peanut butter, chia seeds, and cinnamon in a medium bowl. Stir in the oats, plant milk, maple syrup, if using, and salt, until well combined. Divide the mixture into the two (or three) portions and spoon into mason jars or small bowls with tight-fitting lids. Cover and refrigerate overnight.

2. In the morning, top with pecans and other toppings, if using, and breakfast is served.

Nutrition Analysis

Per serving [for 2 with pecans only]: 510 calories, 14 g protein, 25 g total fat, 58 g carbohydrate, 16 g sugar, 11 g fiber

Per serving [for 3 with pecans only]: 340 calories, 9 g protein, 17 g total fat, 39 g carbohydrate, 11 g sugar, 8 g fiber

Note:

If you prefer your oatmeal hot, you can microwave it in a microwave-safe bowl for a minute to heat through or transfer the oatmeal to a small saucepan and heat for 1 to 2 minutes.

Breakfast Quinoa with Mango and Cashews

Makes 4 servings

2 cups (500 ml) plain unsweetened plant milk

1 cup (170 g) quinoa, well rinsed

2 tablespoons (40 g) pure maple syrup

¼ teaspoon sea salt

1 teaspoon pure vanilla extract

2 large ripe mangoes, peeled, pitted, and chopped, or 2 cups frozen chopped mango, thawed

½ cup (68 g) chopped roasted unsalted cashews

Cashew Cream (page 178) or vegan yogurt, to serve (optional)

Move over oats—quinoa is horning in on your breakfast territory. I'll never forsake my morning oatmeal, but quinoa for breakfast does make a nice protein-rich change of pace, especially with luscious bits of juicy mango and crunchy cashews.

1. Combine the plant milk, quinoa, maple syrup, and salt in a saucepan over high heat. Bring to a boil and reduce to simmer. Cover and simmer for 25 to 30 minutes, until the quinoa is tender.

2. Remove from heat, stir in the vanilla extract, mangoes, and cashews. Cover and set aside for 5 minutes. Serve in bowls topped with cashew cream or vegan yogurt, if using.

Nutrition Analysis

Per serving: 400 calories, 11 g protein, 13 g total fat, 66 g carbohydrate, 31 g sugar, 6 g fiber

Cheesy Mushroom Scramble

Makes 4 to 6 servings

2 tablespoons (30 ml) water, or 1 tablespoon (15 ml) avocado oil

½ cup (80 g) chopped yellow onion

½ red bell pepper, seeded and chopped

1 garlic clove, minced

8 ounces (225 g) mushrooms (any type), cleaned, blotted dry, and thinly sliced or chopped

Sea salt and freshly ground black pepper

12 to 16 ounces (340 to 455 g) extra-firm tofu, drained and crumbled

3 tablespoons (12 g) nutritional yeast

1 teaspoon onion powder

¼ teaspoon turmeric

¼ teaspoon smoked paprika

½ cup (120 ml) Easy Cheesy Sauce (page 44)

The best thing about a tofu scramble (besides being protein rich, delicious, and easy to prepare) is its versatility—mix and match your favorite additions: add chopped vegan sausage or diced cooked potato, if you have some on hand. Leftover cooked veggies are a great addition, too. Serve with whole-grain toast or English muffins for breakfast, lunch, or dinner.

1. Heat the water in a large nonstick skillet over medium heat or spray it with cooking oil spray. Add the onion and bell pepper and cook, stirring occasionally, until soft, 5 minutes. Add the garlic and mushrooms and cook until tender, about 4 minutes. Season with salt and pepper to taste.

2. Combine the crumbled tofu in a mixing bowl with the nutritional yeast, onion powder, turmeric, paprika, and 1 teaspoon of salt. Mix well.

3. Add the tofu mixture to the skillet with the vegetables and cook, stirring, until heated through and well combined. Mix in the cheesy sauce and continue cooking for a few minutes longer. Taste and adjust the seasonings, adding more salt and pepper if needed. Serve hot, drizzled with extra cheesy sauce, if desired.

Nutrition Analysis

Per serving [for 4 (with 12 ounces [340 g] tofu)]: 150 calories, 13 g protein, 6 g total fat, 11 g carbohydrate, 4 g sugar, 2 g fiber

Per serving [for 6 (with 16 ounces [455 g] tofu): 120 calories, 11 g protein, 5 g total fat, 8 g carbohydrate, 2 g sugar, 1 g fiber

Everything Avocado Toast with White Beans and Roasted Tomatoes

Makes 4 to 6 servings

4 to 6 plum tomatoes, halved, seeded, and juiced

2 garlic cloves, thinly sliced

2 teaspoons balsamic vinegar

Sea salt and freshly ground black pepper

1½ cups (266 g) cooked cannellini beans, or 1 (15-ounce [425 g]) can, rinsed and drained

2 avocados, pitted, peeled, and chopped

3 tablespoons (45 ml) fresh lemon juice

3 tablespoons (12 g) chopped fresh parsley

2 tablespoons (5 g) chopped fresh basil leaves

3 scallions, white and green parts, coarsely chopped

4 to 6 slices sprouted whole-grain bread, toasted

Everything Seasoning Mix (page 38)

Avocado toast has gained culinary cult status for a reason—it's delicious! Now you can have your avocado toast—and your plant-protein, too. This recipe amps up the protein with cannellini beans, sprouted whole-grain bread, and a sprinkle of Everything Seasoning. Caramelized roasted tomatoes add a rich flavor.

1. Preheat the oven to 450°F (230°C). Line a rimmed baking sheet with parchment paper or coat lightly with cooking spray.

2. Arrange the tomatoes on the prepared baking sheet, cut side up. Put the garlic in the cavities of the tomatoes, drizzle with balsamic vinegar, and sprinkle lightly with salt and pepper. Lightly press the tomatoes down to flatten.

3. Roast until the tomatoes soften and caramelize, 20 to 25 minutes. Allow them to cool slightly, then carefully remove and discard the skin, if desired. Set aside.

4. In a food processor, combine the beans, avocados, lemon juice, parsley, basil, scallions, and salt and pepper to taste. Process or pulse until smooth or chunky—depending on your preference.

5. To assemble, toast the bread, then divide the avocado mixture evenly among the slices of toast. Top each with two roasted tomato halves and sprinkle with the seasoning mix.

Nutrition Analysis

Per serving [with 4 tomatoes & bread slices]: 320 calories, 13 g protein, 12 g total fat, 43 g carbohydrate, 3 g sugar, 13 g fiber

Per serving [with 6 tomatoes & bread slices]: 240 calories, 10 g protein, 8 g total fat, 35 g carbohydrate, 3 g sugar, 10 g fiber

Peanut Butter and Banana Smoothie

1 large ripe banana, frozen in chunks

2 tablespoons (32 g) creamy natural peanut butter

1 cup (235 ml) plain unsweetened plant milk

1 tablespoon (7 g) hulled hemp seeds

¼ teaspoon ground cinnamon

Smoothies are easy, fast, and perfect for on-the-go nutrition. They're a great way to get a lot of protein and other good-for-you ingredients into your first meal of the day. See a photo of this smoothie on page 135.

1. Combine all of the ingredients in a blender. Blend until smooth.

2. Pour into a glass and serve immediately or refrigerate for up to 24 hours.

Nutrition Analysis

Per serving: 430 calories, 13 g protein, 24 g total fat, 40 g carbohydrate, 18 g sugar, 6 g fiber

Protein and Smoothies

To many people, smoothies are a go-to breakfast or after-work-out snack because they can be an easy and delicious way to get a good amount of protein. One way people get added protein in their smoothies is to add a scoop of vegan protein powder. But it's also easy to add protein to a smoothie without relying on protein powder. For example, you can add some silken tofu, vegan yogurt, nut butter, or nutrient dense seeds, such as hemp seeds, flaxseeds, or chia seeds. You can also use 1 cup (235 ml) plain unsweetened soy milk as the liquid portion of your smoothie for extra eight grams of protein.

PROTEIN PLUS

Almond Butter French Toast

Makes 4 servings

1 cup (235 ml) plain unsweetened plant milk

1 (12-ounce [340 g]) package silken tofu, drained

3 tablespoons (48 g) almond butter

1 teaspoon pure vanilla extract

½ teaspoon ground cinnamon

Pinch of sea salt

8 slices sprouted whole-grain bread

⅓ cup (37 g) toasted slivered almonds

Pure maple syrup, to serve

Start your day with this hearty and delicious French toast made with almond butter and tofu. Top with toasted slivered almonds and maple syrup.

1. Preheat the oven to 200°F (95°C).

2. In a blender, combine the plant milk, tofu, almond butter, vanilla, cinnamon, and salt and blend until smooth. Pour the mixture into a wide, shallow dish.

3. Lightly coat a nonstick skillet with cooking spray and heat over medium-high heat. Dip the bread, one slice at a time, into the batter, letting the excess drain off. Working in batches, place the battered bread in the hot skillet and cook until just browned on the bottom, about 2 minutes, pressing down with a spatula on the center of the bread slices as they cook. Flip and brown the other side, about 2 minutes more. Lower the heat to medium, if needed, to prevent burning. Place the French toast on a heatproof plate and transfer to the oven to keep warm while cooking the remaining French toast.

4. To serve, garnish with almonds and a drizzle of maple syrup.

Nutrition Analysis

Per serving: 390 calories, 17 g protein, 15 g total fat, 49 g carbohydrate, 15 g sugar, 9 g fiber

Chapter 8
Protein-Rich Sweets

Chocolate-Kissed Peanut Butter Pie

Makes 12 servings

Crust

1½ cups (129 g) almond flour

¼ cup (22 g) unsweetened cocoa powder

¼ cup (80 g) pure maple syrup

1 tablespoon (15 ml) neutral-tasting vegetable oil, such as avocado oil , plus more as needed

Filling

1 cup (175 g) vegan semi-sweet chocolate chips, melted

1 (12-ounce [340 g]) package firm silken tofu, drained

1 cup (260 g) creamy natural peanut butter

⅓ cup (106 g) pure maple syrup

1 tablespoon (5 g) unsweetened cocoa powder

2 teaspoons pure vanilla extract

Drizzle

½ cup (88 g) vegan dark chocolate chips

½ teaspoon neutral-tasting vegetable oil, such as avocado oil

¼ cup (36 g) crushed unsalted dry-roasted peanuts

This peanut butter pie is complemented by chocolate because: chocolate. The addition of almond flour and tofu (plus the peanuts and peanut butter, of course) provide a wealth of protein to this decadent treat. If you prefer a firm fudgy texture, keep the pie in the freezer; for a softer, creamier texture, keep it in the refrigerator.

1. Line a 9-inch (23 cm) springform pan with parchment paper.

2. To make the crust, in a food processor, combine the flour, cocoa powder, maple syrup, and oil. Blend until crumbly and well mixed. If the mixture doesn't hold together when pinched between your fingers, add up to 1 tablespoon (15 ml) additional oil. Use your fingers to press the mixture evenly into the bottom and about halfway up the sides of the pan. Place the pan in the freezer while you make the filling.

3. To make the filling, combine all the filling ingredients in a food processor and blend until completely smooth. Pour the filling into the prepared crust and refrigerate or freeze for 4 hours, or until firm.

4. To make the drizzle, in a microwave-safe bowl, combine the chocolate chips and oil. Microwave for 30 seconds, then stir. If not completely melted, microwave again for 10 seconds at a time until melted. Drizzle the melted chocolate over the top of the pie and sprinkle with the crushed peanuts. Store in the refrigerator for up to 3 days or in the freezer for up to 1 month.

Variation:

Try swapping out the peanut butter and peanuts for almond butter and crushed almonds.

Nutrition Analysis

Per serving: 420 calories, 12 g protein, 28 g total fat, 32 g carbohydrate, 22 g sugar, 4 g fiber

Double Chocolate Brownies

1 cup (172) cooked or canned black beans, drained and rinsed

½ cup (160 g) pure maple syrup or agave nectar

¼ cup (64 g) almond butter

3 tablespoons (45 ml) neutral-tasting vegetable oil, such as avocado oil

1 tablespoon (7 g) ground golden flaxseeds, combined with 3 tablespoons (45 ml) hot water

1 teaspoon pure vanilla extract

¾ cup (65 g) almond flour or unbleached all-purpose flour

½ cup (43 g) unsweetened cocoa powder

2 teaspoons baking powder

⅛ teaspoon sea salt

1 to 3 tablespoons (15 to 45 ml) water, as needed

½ cup (87 g) vegan semi-sweet chocolate chips

Double the chocolate (from cocoa and chocolate chips) makes these brownies twice as nice and doubly delicious. Black beans, flaxseeds, and almond flour provide the protein.

1. Preheat the oven to 350°F (180°C). Coat an 8-inch (20 cm) square baking pan with cooking spray or line with parchment paper.

2. In a food processor, combine the black beans, maple syrup, almond butter, oil, flaxseed mixture, and vanilla, and blend until smooth. Add the flour, cocoa powder, baking powder, and salt and process until smooth and well combined. If the batter is too thick to spread easily, add water, 1 tablespoon (15 ml) at a time, and blend again.

3. Scrape the batter into the prepared pan. Sprinkle the chocolate chips on top. Bake for 20 to 25 minutes, until a toothpick comes out clean.

4. Let cool in the pan, then refrigerate for a few hours before cutting into squares.

Nutrition Analysis

Per serving [for 9]: 270 calories, 7 g protein, 17 g total fat, 28 g carbohydrate, 17 g sugar, 5 g fiber

Per serving [for 16]: 150 calories, 4 g protein, 9 g total fat, 16 g carbohydrate, 10 g sugar, 3 g fiber

Nut Lover's Cheesecake

Makes 6 servings

Crust

1 cup (175 g) pitted dates

1 cup (100 g) walnut or pecan piece

Filling

2 cups (60 g) raw cashews, soaked in hot water for 30 minutes, then drained

½ cup (160 g) pure maple syrup or agave nectar

⅓ cup (70 ml) plain unsweetened almond milk or other plant milk

2 teaspoons fresh lemon juice

1½ teaspoons pure vanilla extract

4 tablespoons (64 g) almond butter

Drizzle

2 tablespoons (32 g) almond butter

1 tablespoon (15 ml) neutral-tasting vegetable oil, such as avocado oil

2 tablespoons (28 g) pure maple syrup

Nuts in the crust, nuts in the filling, and an almond butter drizzle on top, make this no-bake cheesecake a nut lover's dream.

1. Coat an 8-inch (20 cm) springform pan with cooking spray or line with parchment paper.

2. In a food processor, combine the dates and walnuts. Blend until finely ground. Transfer the date-walnut mixture into the springform pan and press it evenly into the bottom and halfway up the sides of the pan. Set aside.

3. To make the filling, in a high-speed blender, combine the soaked cashews with the maple syrup, almond milk, lemon juice, and vanilla. Add the almond butter and blend on high until the mixture is very smooth, scraping down the sides as needed. Scrape the filling mixture into the crust and smooth the surface. Place in the freezer for 3 to 4 hours, until firm.

4. To make the drizzle, in a blender or food processor, combine the almond butter, oil, and maple syrup, and blend until smooth.

5. Remove the cheesecake from the freezer about 10 minutes before serving and remove the outer ring of the springform pan. Drizzle with the almond butter drizzle and serve. Store leftovers tightly covered in the freezer for up to 2 weeks.

Nutrition Analysis

Per serving: 550 calories, 8 g protein, 38 g total fat, 51 g carbohydrate, 43 g sugar, 5 g fiber

Two-Seed Chocolate Truffles

1¼ cups (281 g) soft Medjool dates, pitted

½ cup (50 g) walnut pieces, cashews pieces, or other nuts

¼ cup (44 g) chia seeds, plus more if needed

¼ cup (28 g) hulled hemp seeds

¼ cup (22 g) unsweetened cocoa powder, plus more if needed

1 teaspoon pure vanilla extract

3 tablespoons (33 g) vegan semi-sweet chocolate chips, melted

Water (optional)

Ground coconut flakes or ground nuts, to coat (optional)

These little bites are a delicious way to get a protein boost. Pop one or two after a workout or when you need a little burst of energy.

1. Line a rimmed baking sheet with parchment paper and set aside.

2. In a food processor, combine the dates, walnuts, chia seeds, hemp seeds, cocoa powder, and vanilla, and process until smooth and well mixed, scraping down the sides as needed. Add the melted chocolate and process until well combined. The dough should be sticky when pressed between your fingers. If not, add a small amount of water (a teaspoon at a time) and process until it comes together. If the mixture is too wet, add a little more cocoa or chia seeds.

3. Roll the mixture into 1-inch (2.5 cm) balls and arrange on the prepared baking sheet. To coat the truffles, place some cocoa or ground nuts or coconut in a shallow bowl and roll the balls in the coating, then arrange on a plate. Refrigerate until firm, about 1 hour. Cover and store in the refrigerator for up to 3 days.

Nutrition Analysis

Per truffle: 110 calories, 2 g protein, 4.5 g total fat, 18 g carbohydrate, 12 g sugar, 3 g fiber

Almond Butter Blondies

1 cup (164 g) cooked or canned chickpeas, rinsed and drained

½ cup (125 g) almond butter

3 tablespoons (45 ml) neutral-tasting vegetable oil, such as avocado oil

½ cup (160 g) pure maple syrup or agave nectar

2 teaspoons pure vanilla extract

¾ cup (65 g) almond flour or unbleached all-purpose flour

¼ cup (46 g) oat flour

½ teaspoon baking powder

¼ teaspoon baking soda

¼ teaspoon sea salt

¼ teaspoon ground cinnamon

⅓ cup (58 g) vegan chocolate or butterscotch chips (optional)

Water (optional)

Since black beans make great brownies, it's only natural that chickpeas make great blondies, and especially rich blondies at that, thanks to the almond butter. Add the optional chocolate or butterscotch chips—or not, according to your taste.

1. Preheat the oven to 350°F (180°C). Coat an 8-inch (20 cm) square baking pan with cooking spray or line with parchment paper.

2. In a food processor, puree the chickpeas until smooth. Add the almond butter, oil, maple syrup, and vanilla. Process until smooth and well blended.

3. Transfer the chickpea mixture to a bowl. Add the almond flour, oat flour, baking soda, baking powder, salt, and cinnamon, Mix well and fold in the chocolate chips, if using. Scrape the batter into the prepared pan, using a spatula coated with cooking spray to spread the batter evenly. If the batter is too thick to spread easily, add water, 1 tablespoon (15 ml) at a time, and blend again.

4. Bake for 25 minutes, or until a knife inserted in the center comes out clean. Let the blondies cool for 30 minutes before cutting and serving.

Nutrition Analysis

Per serving [for 9]: 260 calories, 7 g protein, 17 g total fat, 23 g carbohydrate, 14 g sugar, 4 g fiber

Per serving [for 16]: 150 calories, 4 g protcin, 10 g total fat, 13 g carbohydrate, 9 g sugar, 2 g fiber

Protein Power Bars

Makes 8 servings

1 cup (175 g) pitted dates

½ cup (60 g) dried cranberries, goji berries, or acai berries

¾ cup (75 g) walnuts or pecans pieces

¾ cup (102 g) cashews or almonds

¾ cup (108 g) sunflower seed kernels

¾ cup (170 g) pumpkin seed kernels (pepitas)

⅓ cup (75 g) almond butter

2 tablespoons (14 g) hulled hemp seeds

Cacao nibs or chopped toasted pumpkin seed kernels, to garnish

This recipe is like a who's-who of nuts, seeds, and dried fruit. The fact is, you can mix and match the specific ingredients to suit your own taste or what you have on hand. The results will be delicious, protein-rich bars that make great snacks or after-dinner treats.

1. Line an 8-inch (20 cm) square baking pan with parchment paper.

2. In a food processor, combine the dates, cranberries, walnuts, and cashews. Process until well mixed. Add the sunflower seeds, pumpkin seeds, almond butter, and hemp seeds. Process until well combined, but still retaining some texture—do not overprocess.

3. Transfer the mixture to the prepared pan, pressing down to distribute it evenly, and smoothing the top. Sprinkle cacao nibs or chopped pumpkin seeds on top, lightly pressing them in into the dough.

4. Refrigerate for 1 hour or longer to firm up before cutting into eight bars measuring 2 inches by 4 inches (5 cm by 10 cm).

Nutrition Analysis

Per serving: 460 calories, 14 g protein, 33 g total fat, 34 g carbohydrate, 21 g sugar, 7 g fiber

Pecan Oatmeal Cookies

Makes 25 to 30 cookies

1 tablespoon (7 g) ground golden flaxseeds, combined with 3 tablespoons (45 ml) hot water

1 cup (125 g) unbleached all-purpose flour

½ cup (43 g) almond flour

1 cup (225 g) packed natural sugar

¾ teaspoon baking soda

½ teaspoon baking powder

¾ teaspoon ground cinnamon

¼ teaspoon sea salt

⅓ cup (70 ml) plain unsweetened plant milk

¼ cup (45 ml) neutral-tasting vegetable oil, such as avocado oil

¼ cup (60 ml) pure maple syrup

1 teaspoon pure vanilla extract

2 cups (312 g) old-fashioned oats

½ cup (55 g) chopped pecans

There's lots to love about these oatmeal cookies made with flaxseeds and almond flour. Chopped pecans add crunch, but you can also add some raisins, dried cranberries, or even chocolate chips, if you're so inclined.

1. Preheat the oven to 350°F (180°C). Line one large rimmed baking sheet with parchment paper or coat with cooking spray.

2. In a large mixing bowl, combine the all-purpose flour, almond flour, sugar, baking powder, baking soda, cinnamon, and salt. Mix to combine well. Add the plant milk, oil, maple syrup, and vanilla and mix until thoroughly combined. Add the oats and pecans and stir to incorporate well. Scoop about 1½ tablespoons (23 ml) of the dough onto one of the prepared baking sheets. Repeat with the remaining dough, spacing them about 2 inches (5 cm) apart. Press down slightly on each dough ball.

3. Bake for 12 minutes, or until golden on the bottom. Let the cookies cool on the pan for about 5 minutes, then use a metal spatula to transfer them to a cooling rack.

Nutrition Analysis

Per cookie [if recipe makes 25]: 130 calories, 2 g protein, 5 g total fat, 19 g carbohydrate, 11 g sugar, 1 g fiber

Per cookie [if recipe makes 30]: 110 calories, 2 g protein, 4.5 g total fat, 16 g carbohydrate, 9 g sugar, 1 g fiber

Banana–Peanut Butter Nice Cream

Makes 4 servings

4 large ripe bananas, peeled, cut into chunks, and frozen (see Note)

½ cup (130 g) creamy natural peanut butter

Chocolate Sauce (see opposite)

Crushed unsalted dry-roasted peanuts, to garnish

The easiest nice cream also happens to be one of the most delicious—just combine frozen bananas and peanut butter in a food processor, and you're in for a treat. The chocolate sauce and crushed peanuts take it over the top.

1. Place the frozen banana chunks in a food processor and process until smooth, scraping down the sides as needed. Add the peanut butter and process to combine. Transfer to a bowl or other container and freeze. For soft-serve ice cream, leave in the freezer for 15 to 20 minutes; for a firmer ice cream, freeze for 2 to 3 hours before serving. If frozen for longer than 4 hours, the ice cream will become hard and should be removed from the freezer for 10 to 15 minutes before serving to soften it slightly.

2. To serve, scoop the ice cream into dessert dishes, spoon the chocolate sauce over top, and sprinkle with peanuts.

Nutrition Analysis

Per serving: 420 calories, 10 g protein, 19 g total fat, 55 g carbohydrate, 32 g sugar, 8 g fiber

Note:

To freeze banana chunks, line a rimmed baking sheet with parchment paper and spread the banana slices on it in a single layer. Freeze for 2 hours. If not using right away, transfer the frozen banana slices to a zipper freezer bag and store in the freezer for up to 1 week.

Chocolate Sauce

Makes 1½ cups (308 ml)

½ cup (160 g) pure maple syrup

½ cup (43 g) unsweetened cocoa powder

¼ cup (60 ml) plain unsweetened plant milk

2 tablespoons (32 g) almond butter

1 teaspoon pure vanilla extract

Drizzle this chocolate sauce over nice cream or use it as a dipping sauce for strawberries or other fruit.

1. Combine all the ingredients in a small saucepan over medium heat, stirring constantly until it is a smooth sauce.

2. Remove from the heat. The sauce will thicken as it cools.

3. Serve warm or at room temperature. If not using right away, cover and refrigerate for up to 1 week, warming it carefully in the microwave before using.

Nutrition Analysis

Per serving: 90 calories, 2 g protein, 3 g total fat, 17 g carbohydrate, 14 g sugar, 2 g fiber

Blueberry Chia Pudding

Makes 3 servings

2 cups (475 ml) plain unsweetened soy or other plant milk

½ cup (88 g) chia seeds

½ cup (120 ml) mashed or pureed fresh or thawed frozen blueberries

2 tablespoons (40 g) pure maple syrup

½ teaspoon pure vanilla extract

Fresh blueberries, to garnish (optional)

In addition to having a high protein content, chia seeds make a great pudding. I like to blend the ingredients in a blender to make a smooth pudding.

1. Combine the soy milk, chia seeds, mashed blueberries, maple syrup, and vanilla in a blender and blend until smooth. Let it sit in the blender for 5 minutes, then blend again.

2. Transfer the pudding to three dessert bowls. Refrigerate for 30 minutes, then stir again. Cover, and refrigerate for 4 hours, or overnight. Serve garnished with fresh blueberries, if using.

Nutrition Analysis

Per serving: 210 calories, 6 g protein, 11 g total fat, 25 g carbohydrate, 11 g sugar, 10 g fiber

Chapter 9
Plant Protein Basics

Beans, Basically

Makes 6 cups (1.4 L)

16 ounces (455g) dried beans

6 to 8 cups (1.4 to 1.8 L) water, plus more if needed

2 bay leaves

2 garlic cloves, crushed

1 to 2 teaspoons sea salt (optional)

One pound (455 g) of dried beans produces about 6 cups (1 kg) cooked. When cooking dried beans it makes sense to cook up a pound at a time, since they take so much time (and energy) to cook. Since they freeze well, they are ideal for portioning and freezing to use as needed. This is a basic template recipe for cooking beans. The actual cooking times will vary, depending on the size and age of the beans used.

1. Soak the beans overnight in water to cover.

2. Drain the beans and put them in a large pot with 6 to 8 cups (1.4 to 1.8 L) of fresh water (older and larger beans require the greater amount of water). Put a lid on the pot and bring to a boil. Reduce the heat to a simmer, add the bay leaves, garlic, and salt, if using, and cook until the beans are tender, 1 to 3 hours, or longer, depending on the bean. Add additional water, if needed, to keep the beans covered while cooking.

3. When the beans are tender, divide them into 2-cup (475 ml) containers and set aside to cool. Once cool, cover with tight-fitting lids and refrigerate some to use right away and freeze the rest.

Beans in a Slow Cooker

Instead of cooking on the stovetop, you can cook the beans in your slow cooker to save energy and free yourself from watching the pot. Simply place the soaked and drained beans in your slow cooker with the water, bay leaves, garlic, and salt, if using. Put on the lid and turn the cooker on Low for 8 to 10 hours.

Beans in a Pressure Cooker

If you have a pressure cooker, you can cook the beans in it, according to the manufacturer's directions.

Braised Tempeh

Makes 8 ounces (225 g)

1 (8-ounce [225 g]) package tempeh

¼ cup (60 ml) tamari

2 cups (475 ml) water

Braising tempeh in liquid helps mellow the flavor of the tempeh and makes it more digestible. I always braise tempeh before using it in recipes. If you'd like to add more flavor, sauté the tempeh first in a little oil with some chopped onion and garlic, then add the water and tamari and simmer.

1. Cut the tempeh to create four ¼-inch (6 mm) thick slices.

2. Combine the tamari and water in a saucepan or deep skillet over medium heat and bring to a boil. Add the tempeh, reduce the heat to low, cover, and simmer for 15 minutes, turning occasionally. Transfer the tempeh to a plate.

3. The tempeh can now be used in recipes or cooled to room temperature, then covered and refrigerated for up to a week.

Nutrition Analysis

Per serving: 220 calories, 23 g protein, 12 g total fat, 9 g carbohydrate, 0 g sugar, 0 g fiber

PROTEIN PLUS

Baked Seitan

This recipe uses vital wheat gluten to make a simple, protein-rich seitan roast that can be enjoyed as is; as a pot roast; or cut it into slices, chunks, or strips for sautés, stews, stir-fries, and more. You can portion and freeze this seitan in airtight containers, with or without the cooking broth.

Makes 20 ounces (567 g)
(6 to 8 servings)

Seitan

1½ cups (432 g) vital wheat gluten flour, plus more if needed

¼ cup (21 g) chickpea flour

3 tablespoons (12 g) nutritional yeast

1½ teaspoons onion powder

1 teaspoon garlic powder

1 teaspoon smoked paprika

¾ teaspoon sea salt

¼ teaspoon freshly ground black pepper

1 cup (235 ml) cold water, plus more if needed

2 tablespoons (30 ml) tamari

1 tablespoon (16 g) white miso paste

1 tablespoon (15 ml) extra-virgin olive oil or water

1 teaspoon browning liquid (Kitchen Bouquet or Gravy Master) (optional)

Cooking Broth

3 cups (710 ml) cold water

2 tablespoons (30 ml) tamari, or 1 teaspoon vegetable broth powder

1. To make the seitan, in a food processor or bowl, combine the vital wheat gluten, chickpea flour, nutritional yeast, onion powder, garlic powder, paprika, salt, and pepper and pulse or stir to mix. Add the water, tamari, miso paste, olive oil, and browning liquid, if using. Process or stir to mix well, until the mixture holds together. If the mixture is too dry to hold together, add a tablespoon (15 ml) or so of water and process or mix to absorb all the flour. If the mixture is too wet to hold its shape, add 1 tablespoon (9 g) of vital wheat gluten and process or mix to incorporate.

2. Transfer the dough to a work surface and knead for about 2 minutes by hand, shaping it into a ball. Cover the dough ball and set aside to rest for a few minutes while you prepare the cooking broth.

3. To prepare the broth, in a measuring cup, combine 1 cup (235 ml) of the water with the tamari and set aside.

4. Preheat the oven to 350°F (180°C). Lightly coat a large sheet of aluminum foil with cooking spray.

5. Form the smooth dough ball into a log about 3 inches (7.5 cm) wide and 8 inches (20 cm) long. Place the roast on the foil and tightly wrap the foil around the roast so it holds its shape. Place the roast in a pan large enough to hold the roast. Pour in the remaining 2 cups (475 ml) of cold water. Cover the roasting pan tightly with aluminum foil. Bake for 45 minutes, then remove the pan from the oven and uncover the pan. Remove the foil from around the roast, leaving the roast and water in the pan. Add the reserved cooking broth mixture to the baking pan. Cover the pan again with the foil, and continue to bake for 45 minutes longer. The cooked seitan should be firm to the touch.

6. If you are using the seitan right away, transfer it to a platter or cutting board and slice with a long serrated knife. If you are not using it right away, allow it cool, then cover and refrigerate until needed, for up to 4 days. The seitan can be cut or sliced to use in recipes. For long-term storage, freeze for up to 3 months.

Seitan in a Slow Cooker

A slow cooker is a great way to cook seitan if you don't want to use the oven. For the seitan roast, oil the inside of a large oval slow-cooker. Pour 1 cup (235 ml) of the cooking broth into the bottom of the pot, then place the loaf-shaped seitan dough in it. Pour in the rest of the broth. Cover with the lid and cook on Low for 6 to 8 hours or on High for 4 hours, turning once halfway through. The cooked seitan should be firm to the touch. Cool and store the seitan as described at left.

Nutrition Analysis

Per 3.3-ounce (94 g) serving [for 6]: 320 calories, 57 g protein, 4 g total fat, 15 g carbohydrate, 1 g sugar, 2 g fiber

Per 2.5-ounce (71 g) serving [for 8]: 240 calories, 43 g protein, 3 g total fal, 11 g carbohydrate, 1 g sugar, 1 g fiber

PROTEIN PLUS

Plant-Perfect Sausage

Makes 6 links

1 (15-ounce [425 g]) can kidney beans, rinsed and drained

3 tablespoons (45 ml) water

2 tablespoons (30 ml) tamari

3 tablespoons (45 ml) extra-virgin olive oil or water

1 cup (144 g) vital wheat gluten, plus more if needed

2 tablespoons (16 g) tapioca starch

1 tablespoon (4 g) nutritional yeast

2 teaspoons smoked paprika

1 teaspoon whole fennel seeds

1 teaspoon ground fennel seeds

½ teaspoon red pepper flakes

1 teaspoon garlic powder

1 teaspoon onion powder

¼ teaspoon cayenne

½ teaspoon sea salt

¼ teaspoon freshly ground black pepper

These sausage links can be sliced or chopped and used as a pizza topping or to add to a scramble. They are also great in a small sub roll with sautéed onions and bell peppers. For less heat, omit the cayenne and cut back on the red pepper flakes.

1. Preheat the oven to 350°F (180°C).

2. In a food processor, combine the kidney beans, water, tamari, and 2 tablespoons (30 ml) of the olive oil and process until well mixed. Add the vital wheat gluten, tapioca starch, nutritional yeast, paprika, whole and ground fennel seeds, red pepper flakes, garlic powder, onion powder, cayenne, salt, and pepper. Process until a soft dough forms. If the dough is too wet to hold its shape, add a little more vital wheat gluten, 1 tablespoon (9 g) at a time.

3. Transfer the dough to a work surface and knead gently for 2 minutes. Divide the dough into six equal pieces. Roll each piece into a link, 6 to 7 inches (15 to 18 cm) long. Place each sausage link on a small sheet of aluminum foil and enclose it in the foil, twisting the ends to seal. Place the foil-wrapped sausage links, seam-side up, in a shallow baking pan; an 8-inch (20 cm) square pan is ideal. Add about ½ inch (1 cm) of water to the pan and cover tightly with foil.

4. Bake for 1 hour, turning the sausages halfway through. Unwrap and cool for about 15 minutes, then refrigerate to firm up, about 1 hour.

5. To cook, heat the remaining 1 tablespoon (15 ml) of olive oil in a skillet over medium heat. Add the sausage links and cook until hot and browned all over, 3 to 5 minutes.

Nutrition Analysis

Per link: 210 calories, 22 g protein, 8 g total fat, 14 g carbohydrate, 1 g sugar, 3 g fiber

170 | The Plant Protein Revolution Cookbook

Tempeh Bacon

Makes 12 to 16 strips

½ (8-ounce [225 g]) package tempeh, cut into thin strips

3 tablespoons (45 ml) tamari

3 tablespoons (60 g) pure maple syrup or agave nectar

2 tablespoons (30 ml) apple cider vinegar

2 tablespoons (30 ml) water

1 teaspoon liquid smoke

½ teaspoon smoked paprika

½ teaspoon freshly ground black pepper

2 tablespoons (30 ml) extra-virgin olive oil

In the vegan food world, "bacon" means smoky, salty, savory, crispy, chewy goodness—no animal flesh needed. Tempeh happens to be a great vehicle for everything we love about bacon. Best of all, it's high in protein and can be easily cut into thin slices for convenience. Use your favorite brand of tempeh—the one I use comes in a long rectangle shape, so I usually cut it in half and end up with two 4-inch (10 cm) squares to cut into thin slices. The actual number of strips you get will depend on how thinly you slice the tempeh. You can wrap the remaining tempeh tightly and refrigerate for another use (or make a second batch of bacon strips!)

1. Arrange the tempeh slices in a shallow baking dish, overlapping slightly if necessary. Set aside.

2. In a small saucepan, combine the tamari, maple syrup, vinegar, water, liquid smoke, paprika, and pepper and heat over medium heat until hot. Pour the hot marinade over the tempeh slices and set aside for 20 minutes to allow the tempeh to absorb the marinade.

3. Heat the olive oil in a large skillet over medium heat. Add the tempeh strips, in batches, and cook, turning once, until the tempeh is nicely browned, about 5 minutes. Pour any remaining marinade onto the tempeh as it cooks and allow it to evaporate.

4. Serve hot. To store, allow the tempeh bacon to cool completely, then transfer to an airtight container and refrigerate for up to 3 days.

Nutrition Analysis

Per strip [if recipe makes 12]: 50 calories, 2 g protein, 3.5 g total fat, 4 g carbohydrate, 3 g sugar, 0 g fiber

Per serving [if recipe makes 16]: 40 calories, 2 g protein, 2.5 g total fat, 3 g carbohydrate, 3 g sugar, 0 g fiber

PROTEIN PLUS

Ham I Am

Protein-rich beans and vital wheat gluten are the main ingredients of this versatile loaf. After baking, it can be chilled and thinly sliced to use in sandwiches and sautés or chopped or diced to use in stews, stir-fries, scrambles, or salads.

Makes about 1½ pounds (680 g)

1 cup (177 g) cooked or canned cannellini or other white beans, well drained

1 cup (235 ml) water, plus more if needed

3 tablespoons (45 ml) tamari

1 tablespoon (16 g) tomato paste

1 tablespoon (15 ml) olive oil or water

1 teaspoon liquid smoke

1½ cups (432 g) vital wheat gluten, plus more if needed

⅓ cup (42 g) unbleached all-purpose flour

¼ cup (16 g) nutritional yeast

2 tablespoons (14 g) tapioca flour or starch

2 teaspoons onion powder

1½ teaspoons garlic powder

1 teaspoon ground coriander

1 teaspoon smoked paprika

½ teaspoon sea salt

¼ teaspoon freshly ground black pepper

⅛ teaspoon ground allspice

1. Preheat the oven to 350°F (180°C).

2. In a food processor, combine the beans, water, tamari, tomato paste, olive oil, and liquid smoke and blend until smooth. Add the vital wheat gluten, flour, nutritional yeast, tapioca flour, onion powder, garlic powder, coriander, smoked paprika, salt, pepper, and allspice. Process to combine and form a soft dough. If the mixture is too wet to hold its shape, add a little more vital wheat gluten, 1 tablespoon (9 g) at a time. If the mixture is dry and crumbly, add a little more water, 1 tablespoon (15 ml) at a time.

3. Transfer to a work surface and knead for 3 minutes, then shape into a loaf, about 9 inches (23 cm) long. Place the loaf on the prepared aluminum foil, roll up in the foil, and twist the ends. Place the loaf in a 10-inch (25 cm) baking dish, seam side up. Add 1 inch (2.5 cm) of water to the baking dish and cover the entire pan tightly with foil.

4. Bake until firm, about 1 hour and 15 minutes. Uncover and allow to cool to room temperature, then refrigerate to firm up for at least 3 hours before slicing to use in recipes.

Nutrition Analysis

Per 4-ounce (113 g) serving: 390 calories, 60 g protein, 4 g total fat, 28 g carbohydrate, 1 g sugar, 5 g fiber

Tofu Bacon

Makes 6 servings

¼ cup (60 ml) tamari

¼ cup (60 ml) water

1 tablespoon (15 g) natural sugar

1 tablespoon (15 g) ketchup

1 tablespoon (4 g) nutritional yeast

1½ teaspoons liquid smoke

½ teaspoon dark sesame oil

12 to 16 ounces (340 to 455 g) extra-firm tofu, drained, pressed, patted dry, and cut lengthwise into ⅛-inch (3 mm) strips

Extra-firm tofu can be used to make tasty bacon slices that are great in sandwiches.

1. Preheat the oven to 350°F (180°C).

2. In a 9 by 13-inch (23 by 33 cm) glass baking dish, combine the tamari, water, sugar, ketchup, nutritional yeast, liquid smoke, and sesame oil. Mix well. Arrange the tofu slices in the marinade in a single layer, overlapping as little as possible. Carefully turn over the tofu to coat with the marinade.

3. Bake for 30 minutes, then carefully turn over the tofu slices with a thin metal spatula. Return them to the oven and continue baking until nicely browned, 20 to 30 minutes longer.

4. Serve hot. To store, all the tofu bacon to cool completely, then transfer to an airtight container and refrigerate for up to 3 days.

Variation:

For crispy bacon that's ready sooner than later, remove the bacon from the oven after the first 30 minutes and pan-fry it in a lightly oiled nonstick skillet for about 2 minutes per side.

Nutrition Analysis

Per serving [12 ounces (340 g) tofu]: 80 calories, 7 g protein, 3.5 g total fat, 5 g carbohydrate, 3 g sugar, 0 g fiber

Per serving [16 ounces (455 g) tofu]: 100 calories, 9 g protein, 4.5 g total fat, 6 g carbohydrate, 3 g sugar, 0 g fiber

Baked Marinated Tofu

¼ cup (60 ml) tamari

3 tablespoons (60 g) pure maple syrup

3 tablespoons (45 ml) fresh lemon juice

2 garlic cloves, minced

1 tablespoon (4 g) nutritional yeast

1 teaspoon onion powder

12 to 16 ounces (340 to 455 g) extra-firm tofu, drained, pressed, patted dry, and cut into ¼-inch (6 mm) thick slices

Marinated baked tofu is widely available in markets, but it can be expensive. It's easy to make your own using extra-firm or super-firm regular tofu (not silken). Enjoy the baked tofu as is or use it in recipes where you need a flavorful tofu, such as in a salad or sandwich.

1. To make the marinade, in a small bowl or blender, combine the tamari, maple syrup, lemon juice, garlic, nutritional yeast, and the onion powder. Mix or blend until well combined.

2. Arrange the tofu slices in a single layer in a large glass or ceramic baking dish. Pour the marinade over the tofu, spreading the marinade with the back of a spoon to cover the tofu. Gently turn the tofu to be sure it is all coated with the marinade. Cover and refrigerate for several hours or overnight.

3. Preheat the oven to 400°F (200°C). Cover a large rimmed baking sheet with parchment paper or coat lightly with cooking spray.

4. Arrange the tofu slices on the prepared baking sheet, pouring the remaining marinade on top of the tofu. Bake for about 30 minutes, or until the tofu is golden brown on both sides, turning once halfway through. Watch carefully near the end of baking time so the marinade does not burn or smoke.

5. Use immediately or cool to room temperature and transfer to a glass or ceramic container, cover, and refrigerate for up to 3 days.

Nutrition Analysis

Per serving [12 ounces (340 g) tofu]: 140 calories, 11 g protein, 4.5 g total fat, 15 g carbohydrate, 11 g sugar, 0 g fiber

Per serving [16 ounces (455 g) tofu]: 170 calories, 14 g protein, 6 g total fat, 16 g carbohydrate, 11 g sugar, 0 g fiber

Butler Soy Curls

Butler Soy Curls are made from whole non-GMO soybeans, so they contain all of the fiber of soy beans, with no additives or preservatives. They are similar to textured soy protein but superior in texture and less processed. They are very tender when reconstituted and great for stir-fries. Since they contain the oil naturally found in soy beans, I keep this dried product in the freezer to avoid rancidity. I use the crumbs on the bottom of the box in the same way as TSP granules. When reconstituted by soaking in hot broth for about 5 minutes, the strips resemble tender chicken (though you can flavor them as you like). I usually recon-stitute more than I am using at that particu-lar time and freeze the remaining for quick meals. Most online vegan stores, including Amazon.com, carry Soy Curls.

Prepared Plant-Protein Alternatives

For quick meals, or times when you're too busy to cook from scratch, you might want to try various brands of meaty vegan products, such as meaty strips, roasts, sausages, and more. These products are generally made from a combination of soy and wheat proteins Common brands are Gardein, Yves, Lightlife, Morningstar Farms, and White Wave. They are available in natural food stores and large supermarkets, either refrigerated or frozen. Some online vegan vendors will ship them with cold packs.

Cashew Cream

Makes about 1 cup (235 ml)

1 cup (30 g) raw cashew pieces, soaked in hot water for 15 minutes, then drained

½ cup (120 ml) water, plus more if needed

Cashew cream is made the same way you make cashew milk, only using less water. The thick creamy goodness that is cashew cream is a revelation and makes magic happen in many vegan recipes.

1. Combine the drained cashews and water in a high-speed blender. Add the water and blend until completely smooth and creamy. The cashew cream should be very thick. For a thinner cream, add a little more water, 1 tablespoon (15 ml) at a time.

2. Transfer to a bowl with a tight-fitting lid and chill until ready to serve. It will keep well in the refrigerator for up to 3 days.

Nutrition Analysis

Per 2-tablespoon (30 ml) serving: 20 calories, 1 g protein, 1.5 g total fat, 1 g carbohydrate, 0 g sugar, 0 g fiber

Cashew Sour Cream

Makes about 1 cup (235 ml)

¾ cup (23 g) raw cashews, soaked in hot water for 30 minutes, then drained

⅓ cup (70 ml) plain unsweetened plant milk

2 tablespoons (30 ml) rice vinegar

1 tablespoon (15 ml) neutral-tasting vegetable oil, such as avocado oil

⅛ teaspoon sea salt

This plant-based sour cream delivers a creamy texture and a just-tart-enough flavor. Use it to top baked potatoes or in any recipe calling for sour cream.

1. Combine the drained cashews, plant milk, vinegar, oil, and salt in a high-speed blender and blend until very smooth. Transfer the mixture to a container, cover tightly, and refrigerate for at least 2 hours to chill and thicken before use. Keep refrigerated for 3 to 4 days.

Nutrition Analysis

Per 2-tablespoon (30 ml) serving: 35 calories, 1 g protein, 3 g total fat, 1 g carbohydrate, 0 g sugar, 0 g fiber

Tofu
Sour Cream

Makes 1 cup (235 ml)

6 ounces (168 g) soft silken tofu, drained

1½ tablespoons (23 ml) fresh lemon juice

1 tablespoon (15 ml) neutral-tasting oil, such as avocado oil

½ teaspoon sea salt

¼ teaspoon natural sugar (optional)

This sour cream alternative couldn't be easier to make. Blend in some minced chives and try it on baked potatoes, or use it in recipes calling for sour cream.

1. Combine all the ingredients in a food processor or blender and process until smooth and creamy.

2. Transfer to a container with a tight-fitting lid.

3. Cover and refrigerate until you are ready to use it, up to 3 to 4 days.

Nutrition Analysis

Per 2-tablespoon (30 ml) serving: 30 calories, 1 g protein, 2.5 g total fat, 1 g carbohydrate, 0 g sugar, 0 g fiber

Cashew Mayonnaise

Makes 1 cup (235 ml)

⅔ cup (20 g) raw cashews, soaked in hot water for 30 minutes, then drained

⅓ cup (70 ml) plain unsweetened plant milk

2 tablespoons (30 ml) rice vinegar

1 tablespoon (15 ml) fresh lemon juice

¾ teaspoon sea salt

½ teaspoon mustard powder

3 tablespoons (45 ml) avocado oil or other neutral-tasting oil

To add an eggy flavor to your mayonnaise, add a pinch of kala namak (Himalayan black salt) to the mixture.

1. Combine the drained cashews with the plant milk, vinegar, lemon juice, salt, and mustard powder in a high-speed blender and blend until smooth. Let the mixture sit for 5 minutes.

2. With the machine running, slowly pour in the avocado oil in a thin stream, blending until very smooth. Taste and adjust the seasonings, if needed.

3. Transfer the mixture to a bowl or jar with a tight-fitting lid and refrigerate for at least 30 minutes to thicken. This mayo will keep well in the refrigerator for about 1 week.

Nutrition Analysis

Per 2-tablespoon (30 ml) serving: 60 calories, 1 g protein, 7 g total fat, 1 g carbohydrate, 0 g sugar, 0 g fiber

Soy Mayonnaise

Makes 1½ cups (355 ml)

1 (12-ounce [340 g]) package extra-firm silken tofu, drained

2½ tablespoons (38 ml) rice vinegar

1 tablespoon (15 ml) avocado oil (optional)

1 teaspoon sea salt

½ teaspoon mustard powder

Pinch of natural sugar (optional)

This is a protein-rich version of the versatile condiment that is naturally cholesterol-free. Use it as a sandwich spread or in salad dressing. If you prefer the convenience of store-bought, plant-based mayonnaises can be found in natural food stores and supermarkets.

1. Combine all of the ingredients in a food processor or blender and blend until very smooth. Taste and adjust the seasonings, if needed.

2. Transfer the mayo to a glass jar or other container with a tight-fitting lid.

3. Cover tightly, and refrigerate until needed, up to a week.

Nutrition Analysis

Per 2-tablespoon (30 ml) serving: 15 calories, 2 g protein, 0.5 g total fat, 1 g carbohydrate, 0 g sugar, 0 g fiber

Cashew Cream Cheese

Makes 1 cup (235 ml)

¾ cup (20 g) raw cashews, soaked in hot water for 15 minutes, then drained

3 tablespoons (45 ml) neutral-tasting vegetable oil, such as avocado oil

1 tablespoon (15 ml) plain unsweetened plant milk

1 tablespoon (15 ml) rice vinegar

1 tablespoon (15 ml) fresh lemon juice

½ teaspoon sea salt

Use in recipes calling for cream cheese. For an herbed cream cheese, add 1 to 2 tablespoons (4 to 8 g) of minced fresh herbs—I like a combination of parsley, chives, and dill—and serve as a dip or spread.

1. Combine all the ingredients in a high-speed blender and blend until completed smooth and creamy.

2. Transfer the mixture to a bowl or jar with a tight-fitting lid.

3. Cover and refrigerate for at least 2 hours to chill and thicken before use. It will keep well in the refrigerator for up to 5 days.

Nutrition Analysis

Per 2-tablespoon (30 ml) serving: 60 calories, 0 g protein, 6 g total fat, 1 g carbohydrate, 0 g sugar, 0 g fiber

Further Reading

Barnard, Neal D., M.D. *The Vegan Starter Kit: Everything You Need to Know About Plant-Based Eating.* New York: Grand Central Publishing, 2018.

Campbell, T. Colin, PhD. and Campbell, Thomas M. Campbell, II. *The China Study: Startling Implications for Diet, Weight Loss, and Long-term Health.* Dallas, TX: BenBella, rev. ed., 2016.

Frazier, Matt. *No Meat Athlete, Revised and Expanded: A Plant-Based Nutrition and Training Guide for Every Fitness Level—Beginner to Beyond.* Beverly, MA: Fair Winds Press, 2nd ed., 2018.

Fuhrman, Joel, M.D. *Eat to Live: The Amazing Nutrient-Rich Program for Fast and Sustained Weight Loss.* Boston: Little, Brown and Company (Hachette), rev. ed., 2011.

Greger, Michael, M.D. *How Not to Die: Discover the Foods Scientifically Proven to Prevent and Reverse Disease.* New York: Flatiron Books, 2015.

Roll, Rich. *Finding Ultra (Revised and Updated): Rejecting Middle Age, Becoming One of the World's Fittest Men, and Discovering Myself.* New York: Harmony Books, 2013.

Stone, Gene, ed. *Forks Over Knives: The Plant-Based Way to Health.* New York: The Experiment, 2011.

Acknowledgments

About the Author

I'm grateful beyond measure to Eve-Marie Williams, who once again rose to the challenge of testing a huge number of recipes in a short amount of time. You deserve a medal, but I hope you'll settle for my heartfelt thanks.

I also want to thank Sandy Tyrie, Brandie Bloggins, Kimberly Mansfield, and Robin Fetter, who also tested recipes for this book.

Many thanks to the team at Quarto/The Harvard Common Press, including Meredith Quinn, Anne Re, and Todd Conly, for helping to make this book a reality, and especially Dan Rosenberg for recognizing the need for this book and for thinking of me for the project.

My continuing gratitude goes to my longtime literary agent, Stacey Glick of Dystel, Goderich, and Bourret.

Finally, and foremost, heaps of love and appreciation go to my husband, Jon, and my fabulous felines, for their continued love and support.

Robin Robertson has worked with food for more than thirty years as a restaurant chef, cooking teacher, and food writer. A longtime vegan, Robin is the author of more than twenty-five cookbooks, including the best-selling *Vegan Planet*, *Fresh from the Vegan Slow Cooker*, *One-Dish Vegan*, *1000 Vegan Recipes*, *Quick-Fix Vegan*, and *Vegan Mac & Cheese*.

Robin has written regular columns for *VegNews Magazine* and *Vegetarian Times*, as well as feature articles for *Cooking Light*, among others. In addition to writing her own cookbooks, she has written the recipes for several well-known authors, including *The How Not to Die Cookbook, and The How Not to Diet Cookbook*, follow-up cookbooks to Dr. Michael Greger's bestselling books.

Robin is active on social media including Facebook, Twitter, Instagram, and Pinterest. Her website is **www.robinrobertson.com.**

Index